The Big Fight

Dave Hannigan is a reporter with Ireland's *Sunday Tribune*, for whom he writes a weekly column on sport in America. A former young journalist of the year, he co-produced 'They Called Him God', a television biography of Paul McGrath, named best sports programme in the 1999 National Media Awards. Born in Cork, he currently lives in New York with his wife Cathy and son Abe.

THE BIG FIGHT

DAVE HANNIGAN

YELLOW JERSEY PRESS
LONDON

Published by Yellow Jersey Press 2002

2 4 6 8 10 9 7 5 3 1

Copyright © Dave Hannigan 2002

Dave Hannigan has asserted his right under the Copyright, Designs
and Patents Act 1988 to be identified as the author of this work

First published in Great Britain in 2002 by
Yellow Jersey Press
Random House, 20 Vauxhall Bridge Road, London SW1V 2SA

Random House Australia (Pty) Limited
20 Alfred Street, Milsons Point, Sydney,
New South Wales 2061, Australia

Random House New Zealand Limited
18 Poland Road, Glenfield,
Auckland 10, New Zealand

Random House South Africa (Pty) Limited
Endulini, 5A Jubilee Road, Parktown 2193, South Africa

The Random House Group Limited Reg. No. 954009
www.randomhouse.co.uk

A CIP catalogue record for this book is available from the British Library

ISBN 0-224-06306-5

Papers used by The Random House Group are natural,
recyclable products made from wood grown in sustainable forests; the manufacturing processes
conform to the environmental regulations of the country of origin

Typeset by SX Composing DTP, Rayleigh, Essex
Printed and bound in Great Britain by
Biddles Ltd., Guildford & Kings Lynn

Contents

To the memory of my grandmother, Christina Morrissey

Acknowledgements

In the summer of 1997, I spent a hugely enjoyable afternoon in the company of Paddy Monaghan, listening to the tale of his extraordinary relationship with Muhammad Ali. On the way out the door, he handed me a copy of his autobiography, and it was reading that book which first made me think that Ali's visit to Dublin might warrant a publication of its own. Four years on, I casually mentioned the idea to Will Buckley, and he fulfilled a bar-stool promise to introduce me to Rachel Cugnoni at Yellow Jersey Press, whose subsequent enthusiasm and support for this project was infectious.

Every single person I rang was only too eager to be interviewed and for being so liberal with their time, and in many cases, dredging their memories to recall incidents from nearly three decades ago, I am deeply indebted to: Joe Brereton, Sean Brereton, Rock Brynner, Paddy Byrne, Gerry Callan, Tim Conn, John Conteh, Mick Daly, Paddy Doherty, Terry Downes, Mickey Duff, Angelo Dundee, Barney Eastwood, Don Elbaum, Steve Eisner, Arlynne Eisner, George Francis, Elgy Gillespie, Pete Hamill, Colin Hart, Thomas Hauser, Alan Hubbard, Eddie Keher, Dr. Stuart Kirschenbaum, Al 'Blue' Lewis, Paddy Maguire, Bernadette McAliskey, John McCormack, Pat McCormack, Paddy Monaghan, John Murphy, Thomas Myler, Ulick O'Connor, Cathal O'Shannon, Antoinette O'Brien (Clare Heritage Centre), John O'Shea, Bill Shorten, Budd Schulberg, Gerry Thornley, Jose Torres, Isabelle Warnas.

A sizeable research load was significantly lightened by contributions from: PJ Browne, John Burns, Peter Carbery, Shane Coleman, Tom English, Deirdre Flood (Croke Park Museum), Liam Horan, Fergal Keane, Steve Lott, Kenneth

ix

McDermott, Robert McDermott, Enda McEvoy, Fleur Muldowney, John O'Brien, Paul Rowan, Liam Ryan, Ger Siggins, Mary Smith and Marie Toft. At the *Sunday Tribune*, the patience of the editor Matt Cooper and sports editor Mark Jones made the last six months a lot easier than it might have been.

For supporting me in various ways over the past while, I'd like to express my gratitude to: Plunkett Carter, Fergus Cassidy, Tommy Conlon, Keith Cooney, Ken Cotter, Michelle DiCicco, Keith Gamache, Paul and Tracy Gamblin, Rory Godson, John Haughey, Bob Hennessy, Deirdre McCarthy, Mike and Ginger McGinty, Gavin O'Connor, Mark O'Loughlin, Mark Penney, Gary Ring, Gus Roche, Guy Sarfati and Ciaran Spillane.

Emmet Barry, Paul Howard, Michael Moynihan, Gary Murphy, Colm O'Callaghan and Denis Walsh answered every desperate request for assistance above and beyond the call of duty, and it is a privilege to call each of them my friend.

Since moving to America two years ago, George and Clare Frost and their family have been a constant source of encouragement. For playing that role in my life over a much longer period, and for everything else they have given me, I want to thank my brother, Tom, sisters, Denise and Anne, and niece Kadie Pearse.

My mother and father, Denis and Theresa, are extraordinary people to whom I owe a debt that can never be repaid. I would like to pay special tribute also to my wife Cathy, without whose love and understanding, my life would be a much lesser place; and to my son Abe for teaching me how much fun we can have together at five in the morning, every morning.

If I left anybody out, I apologise now, and any mistakes are of course my own.

Dave Hannigan

Rocky Point, New York, March 2002

Prologue

In the 19th century, there was a place in West Clare known only as 'The Rock of the Weeping of the Tears'. Entire families would journey to this awful landmark to say their last goodbyes to a son or daughter, brother or sister, who was emigrating. At 'The Rock', they would turn back for home, knowing the chances they would ever see the departing relative again were almost nil. Between 1850 and 1880, 100,000 people left the county for America in search of improved circumstances, greater opportunity and a better life. The price of passage was around one pound, and the haunting memory of the wailing farewell.

The Gradys lived in the Turnpike, an area of Ennis town where families subsisted in one and two room single-storey dwellings heaped on top of each other. John Grady was a plasterer who rented a house and a small garden with a rateable value of 15 shillings. Sometime in the 1860s, his son Abe cobbled together the fare for a ticket to the new world and as with so many of his contemporaries, he most likely walked the 30 miles from Ennis to the deepwater Port of Cappa near Kilrush.

Back then, the huge vessels which ferried cotton from New Orleans to Liverpool used to stop off at Cappa on their way back across the Atlantic. Having replaced the cotton with less bulky manufactured goods in their hold, they had plenty of room to take on passengers willing to endure the extra hardship of traversing the ocean in a cargo ship. Conditions were uniformly appalling but it was the cheapest way to travel and an important factor in persuading the poorest sections of Irish society to try their luck in Louisiana rather than New York.

Once in New Orleans, it is believed that Abe Grady gradually worked his way up the Mississippi River before finally settling in Kentucky. There, he met and married an emancipated slave woman whose name is not known. Around 1887, the couple had a son and called him John Lee Grady in a nod to his paternal grandfather back home in Clare. In 1914, John L. also married an African-American, Birdie Moorehead, and they had two children of their own. A son named after his father was born in 1915, and on February 12, 1917, Birdie had a daughter, Odessa Lee.

Odessa Lee Grady grew up in Louisville where she subsequently met, fell in love with, and married a sign-painter, Cassius Marcellus Clay Sr. At 6.35 pm on January 17, 1942 in Louisville General Hospital, she gave birth to a son. They called him Cassius Marcellus Clay Jr., but by the time he set foot in Ireland for the first time just over thirty years later, the world knew him only as Muhammad Ali.

If You're Irish, Come into the Parlour

By the age of twenty-four, Rock Brynner, son of Yul, had earned a master's in philosophy from Trinity College, Dublin, performed his one-man adaptation of Jean Cocteau's *Opium* on the Broadway stage, and embarked on a tour of Europe in the guise of a street performer named Red Hat the Clown. In 1971, his travels took him to Switzerland where he met Hans-Rudi Jaggi, a rock impresario, whose efforts to bring Ali to fight in Zurich were being hampered by his own poor grasp of English. Notwithstanding his father naming him after Rocky Graziano, Brynner's association with boxing had extended no further than once successfully wagering a semester's allowance that Cassius Clay would beat Sonny Liston. Good call.

Still, he spoke the language, and for Jaggi, that was the only qualification that counted. Having been hired as translator, Brynner was clued in enough to know that for an outsider the best route to Ali lay through the New York publicist Harold Conrad. From a phone in Conrad's Manhattan offices, he contacted Ali's manager, Herbert Muhammad, about the possibility of a fight in Switzerland, and was invited to meet with both men in Houston before the Jimmy Ellis fight. Through Brynner's intercession, Jaggi, Conrad and Muhammad eventually put together the forgettable bout with Jürgen Blin. It was an incident the day before Ali knocked Ellis out in the twelfth, however, that caused Brynner's own life to take a delightful left turn.

'We were on our way to a training session and the rest of entourage had rushed ahead to sell photos and merchandise and the like,' says Brynner. 'Muhammad stayed behind and he and I ended up going off together for a walk. We were walking along when suddenly this very large Texan redneck came up and started shouting all kinds of racist insults at him, asking things like: "Hey, nigger, why don't you go back to Vietnam?" It had only been a couple of months since the Supreme Court ruled that all charges against him for refusing induction in the army were to be dropped, and this thug was shouting and roaring and Muhammad just danced away from him.

'But this guy kept coming at him and then started throwing some punches. Now, Muhammad couldn't lift a finger or he'd lose his licence to box again so he kept dancing away from him, telling me: "Just keep moving, don't pay him no mind." But the guy kept coming. Finally, I surprised myself. Remembering a trick my father had taught me once, I grabbed the guy's hand and bent it back, breaking two of his fingers. He dropped to the ground in agony and Muhammad and I waltzed away from the scene. After a minute or so, Muhammad turned to me and said, "Who'd have ever thunk the son of the Pharaoh of all Egypt would be protecting a little black boy from Louisville?"'

From then on, Brynner was Ali's bodyguard. It was a loose arrangement that suited everybody involved. There was no salary, no contract. Nothing as coarse as that. When a fight was on, Brynner answered the call and everything else would already be in place. A plane ticket at the airport. A hotel room when he arrived. He spent more than four years travelling the globe as a member of the extended Ali family. Not one of those who were there at the beginning or at the end. Just somebody who found himself in a peculiar situation and hitched along for the most unbelievable ride.

A few months after the Blin fight, Conrad tracked Brynner down in London to tell him that – in conjunction with Butty Sugrue, an Irish publican with a background in the circus – he was trying to bring Ali to fight in Dublin. At the precocious age of sixteen Brynner had transferred from Yale to Trinity College and, after graduation, he stayed on in the city to premiere *Opium* at the Dublin Theatre Festival. It was a town that held nothing but good memories for him, and despite initially regarding Ali and Dublin as a potentially awkward mix, the more he thought about that unlikely combination, the more excited he became at the chance of revisiting his old stomping ground in such exalted company.

'I had one real wish beforehand,' says Brynner. 'I wanted to walk into my old college pub, the Old Stand, with Muhammad. I'd spent many of my undergraduate years in that pub and would always drop in when visiting Dublin so I knew the barmen and they knew me. Muhammad being Muhammad, he was only too happy to do it. I actually got to walk in there, not only with Muhammad Ali, which was great in itself, but the fact I was walking in as his bodyguard was just funny. The barmen remembered me but still acted very nonchalant when they saw us. They looked at us as if all along they expected Muhammad Ali, the most famous man in the world, to walk into their bar. We didn't stay in the Old Stand very long but he was happy to do it because he knew it was something I wanted to do.'

Throughout his spell as bodyguard, Brynner looked nothing like the burly men in suits and shades that accompany today's celebrities. He was, as he put it himself, in full hippie garb in those years. Six inches smaller and eighty pounds lighter than the man he was minding, Brynner had lengthy hennaed hair usually set off by a gold earring. His fingernails were grown deliberately long to assist his playing of a twelve-string guitar on which he tried in vain to teach Ali some rudimentary chords. Among his outlandish outfits for that particular week in Dublin was an ensemble consisting of a garish pink floppy hat, a long red crochet vest and white flared trousers. He often carried with him a small, Gladstone bag, replete with Indian scarf wrapped around the handle, and enigmatically told enquiring journalists that the bag contained the answers to all the world's problems.

Deducing that his local knowledge, if not his dress sense, might be a potentially valuable asset in Ireland, Conrad made sure that this exotic young blade, whom he occasionally referred to as 'that strange-looking kook', was part of his advance party once the fight was set up. So, when the flight carrying Ali touched down at Dublin airport just before ten on Tuesday morning of 11 July, Brynner was already working hard. Before anybody deplaned, he was up the steps carrying a suitcase full of jackets. Subscribing to the old American belief that there is no greater compliment you can pay the Irish than to wear green on St Patrick's Day, Brynner handed every member of the Ali entourage an emerald-coloured blazer.

As the crowd milled around the bottom of the steps, Angelo Dundee was first to emerge. A bespectacled, dark-haired man, he looked like nothing else as much as somebody arriving from America on business. Which of course he was. He dawdled a few moments at the top of the steps. In a dozen years as Ali's trainer, Dundee knew better than to walk down the stairs first and upstage the headline act. Finally, the hulking figure of Ali appeared at the door of the plane and stepped forward, his right hand raised in acknowledgement of the people gathered to witness his arrival.

The music of the Emerald Girls' Pipe Band strained across the wide expanse of the runway as, wide-eyed and beaming that familiar, effervescent grin, Ali walked slowly down the stairway. With every step, more and more of his entourage emerged from the darkness of the plane door, their leader moving at a pace that allowed the spectators a proper look at somebody the vast majority of them had only ever seen through the wonders of the cathode ray tube.

No sooner had he reached the bottom step, where two Aer Lingus hostesses stood smiling sentry, than he met his first opportunistic Irish politician. Timothy 'Chubb' O'Connor, a Teachta Dála (TD) representing Kerry North and a good friend of the co-promoter, Butty Sugrue, ambushed Ali on the tarmac, handing the bemused visitor a shillelagh. A walking stick said to represent the staunch spirit and perseverance of the Irish, Ali took the shillelagh in his hand, pondered on its design and then swung it like a hammer. Everybody laughed.

If he was tired after the transatlantic flight, it didn't show. Even before the press formalities began, he was in sparkling form. When Sugrue introduced him to Denis Murphy, and explained that the Laois man was in charge of ticket sales for the fight, Ali responded: 'You're the man I'll have to look after in Ireland.' Ignoring the fact that his fee was guaranteed regardless of the box-office takings, this was Ali at his most charming, giving every stranger he met exactly what they wanted. One throw-away line from him, one precious memory for Murphy of the day he breathed the same air as a sporting giant.

'Ali's Irish debut took place in the huge jumbo arrivals pavilion at Dublin airport yesterday morning,' wrote Sean Diffley in the following day's *Irish Press*. 'There to bear witness to the occasion were scores of early-rising newspapermen, hordes of television and radio technicians and interviewers, several platoons of public relations people, promoters, match-makers, police, security men and the entire staff of Aer Lingus International! Only himself could command such attention. The arc lamps glared, the cameras clicked, the spectators stared and Ali quipped.'

Those members of the public without the necessary connections to gain access to the tarmac gathered inside the arrivals hall. Most estimates reckon there were six hundred people waiting there specifically to catch a glimpse. On more than one occasion, they passed a few minutes by breaking into sustained chants of 'Al-ee, Al-ee, Al-ee'. Their patience would be taxed still further because in another part of the building, every journalist and photographer who could find an excuse to be there was present for the start of Ali's first press conference.

Figuring that Ali's Irish ancestry was a trump card waiting to be played but also realising that the man himself mightn't be too fond of discussing the 'white' branches on his family tree, Conrad had already discreetly told a couple of reporters the story of Abe Grady. Unfortunately, he had neglected to warn them about how best to phrase any questions on the subject. Once Ali heard the name Cassius Clay used by one inquisitor, he narrowed his eyes, turned his head to look away and then launched into a diatribe that had become familiar in the eight years since he stopped answering to Clay.

'Why do you call me Clay? Clay is a slave name I was given. What would you think of a Chinaman called John Weisenstein?'

The assembled press corps must have thought he was set to give them more than they bargained for when he showed his darker side so early in the exchanges. In a nation where American politicians had set great store in coming back to trace and, on occasion, exaggerate their roots, they were not accustomed to a response summed up by the headline in the following day's *Daily Mail*: CLAY GETS ALI'S IRISH BLOOD UP.

'After a couple of questions about the usual stuff, Raymond Smith pipes up,' says John O'Shea, who covered Ali's arrival for the *Evening Press*. "There is a rumour going around that you had an Irish relation. Which part of Ireland was he or she from and could you be specific?" I think it was the only time in his life that Muhammad Ali was stuck for a word. He looked as if to say, "Who let your man out?" We all broke into stitches, and Ali genuinely looked gobsmacked.'

Ali knew enough about his family background – later in the week he would confirm to the *New York Times* that his grandmother's name was Grady – not to have been surprised by the question. However, he was then in his radical Nation of Islam phase, preaching a black separatist ideology, and so he answered in general terms by addressing the issue of nineteenth-century slave owners taking advantage of the slave women. In doing so, he did Abe Grady something of a disservice.

According to the research of Isabelle Warnas at the Family History Library in Utah, Grady married a freed slave woman in the 1870s or early 1880s in Kentucky. Even in post-Civil War America, this was a time when the Irish were known as 'white Negroes' and blacks were commonly referred to as 'smoked Irish'. It is fair to assume then that the couple did not have things easy. As per the racial politics of the era, their son John Lee Grady, born circa 1887, would have been classified as 'mulatto', the term used to described anybody born of one white and one black parent. Just because it didn't suit his own orthodoxy in

1972, Ali is guilty at the very least of simplifying a very complex facet of his heritage.

The best we can say in his defence perhaps is that he may not have known the full Grady story at the time. Warnas didn't present him with her comprehensive version of his family tree until 1989, and when he was growing up, the Grady side of the family didn't figure all that much. Ali's grandmother Birdie Grady had divorced John Lee in the late 1920s and moved 150 miles from Hopkins' County to Louisville. That she brought her kids to a new city far (150 miles then was far) from their father suggests that the break-up was not amicable. That the extended family have always claimed to know very little about the Gradys also supports this contention.

In his own autobiography, *The Greatest*, ghosted by Richard Durham, edited by Toni Morrison, and published three years after his visit to Ireland, Ali claimed to have 'very little knowledge, if any' of 'white blood' in his family. He postulated that this was more evidence of a widespread practice involving whites trying to denigrate blacks who achieve greatness by always claiming they were partly white. His contention was that only criminal or destitute blacks were ever classified as what he called 'pure black'.

Fortunately for his popularity in Dublin, Ali extricated himself from a potentially damaging situation that morning by delivering a memorable line about his possible Irishness that the journalists could run with for the next day's papers.

'You can never tell,' he said, grinning. 'There was a lot of sneakin' around in them days.'

It wasn't the most auspicious of starts, but the mood in the room improved when matters turned to less controversial subjects, like his seventh round knockout of Jerry Quarry in Las Vegas just two weeks earlier.

'You gotta remember that some guys lose heart when I beat them, but it's no disgrace,' he said. 'I'm the greatest . . . It's hard to be modest when you're as good as I am.' The audience erupted laughing. This was what they had come to see.

Joe Frazier came in for his standard ration of abuse. Asked whether he was now better equipped to depose the champion, Ali picked up the shillelagh, waved it over his head and answered: 'I'll whup him easy now.' After a theatrical pause to allow the guffawing to subside, he was off and running. 'I am better now that I ever was in my whole career. I draw the people and Frazier does not want to meet me because he knows it will be his last big date . . . Frazier is too ugly to be champion. He was so ugly after his last fight that his face should have been donated to the Bureau of Wildlife.'

Somebody had the temerity to mention a then growing belief that Frazier might never entertain the idea of a rematch, but Ali didn't take the bait. 'Money rules the world,' he said. 'The whole world wants this repeat and it will be the greatest ever in the history of the planet Earth. Money talks and Frazier has seven children and another on the way so the big one will come off.'

Danny McAlinden, an Irish heavyweight prospect at the time, also cropped up in discussions. Not a name that would have meant much to Ali, he was still polite enough to use the suggestion of a future bout between the pair as comic fodder. 'If he's crazy enough to fight me – I'll fight him,' he said, before quickly adding, 'If he even dreamed he'd beat me, he'd better wake up and apologise now!'

It wasn't all bravado.

'I do not know the reason why there are shootings and killings up there,' said Ali, responding very sensibly to a question about the continued troubles in Northern Ireland. 'When you do not know the reason, it is not wise to comment. It all seems very headachy and very scary. I just like to take care of things in my own area.'

On the subject of his immediate opponent, he tempered his comments, knowing he had a job to sell the forthcoming show. 'It will be a tough fight because Al "Blue" Lewis is a good boy, naturally not the best, but one of the best, and I'd like to give the people of Ireland a good show.'

This was the way of it for much of the press conference.

Journalists attempted to put new spins on questions he'd been asked a thousand times in the past, and he dutifully recycled adaptations from his plentiful stock of witty answers and hilarious put-downs.

'It was a remarkable performance,' wrote Diffley in the *Irish Press*. 'His timing is as cold-bloodedly impeccable as vintage Bob Hope or Sammy Davis. The only discernible difference is that Ali is much the prettier. He was tired and perhaps a bit bored. It had all happened so often before – but he masked his feelings like the real pro and launched into the old routine. Almost every answer brought a hail of laugher. There is no lack of subtlety about Muhammad Ali inside or outside the ring.'

Towards the end of the press conference, Ali gave further proof that his mood hadn't been dented too much by hearing himself referred to as Clay. Whether somebody in his party had fed him this line on the plane over, or whether he was genuinely intrigued by the sheer whiteness of the crowds he encountered during that first hour in Ireland, he brought the house down when apropos of nothing in particular, he mused aloud. 'By the way, I've never been in this country before. I don't know it very well. Where do all the coloured folk hang out?'

On that note, it remained only for Ali and his party to be guided through the throng of pale-skinned fans lurking in the main arrivals area. He then clambered into the back seat of a black chauffeur-driven Mercedes to be taken right through the city, out into the foothills of the Dublin mountains to his hotel. Built at a cost of nearly a million pounds, Opperman's Country Club had been opened just three weeks earlier by Willy and Johnny Opperman, the sons of a Swiss chef who had emigrated to Ireland decades earlier. Ten miles from the centre of the city, much too far and inconvenient for many gawping fans to make the pilgrimage, it appeared the perfect remove for a fighter preparing to do battle. There was even a squad car containing two Gardai posted at the entrance as an extra deterrent.

Within a week, of course, Ali would grow tired of the sedate atmosphere and complain bitterly about there being 'no action' around his hotel. Angelo Dundee loved Opperman's idyllic location – one of his fondest memories of the entire trip is of the long, scenic walks he took with his wife Helen and daughter Teri. While Teri Dundee made full use of the horse-riding facilities nearby, Ali was bored. For somebody who thrived on the oxygen of attention, he hated the fact that, unlike almost every other hotel he stayed at, the lobby wasn't full of visitors loitering in the singular hope of seeing him. The ever-present posse of journalists could only fill that role for so long. That first morning, however, he had yet to discover anything bad about Opperman's and ever the good pro, he repaired straight to bed to offset the jet lag.

'Me and my buddy Alan Hubbard had missed the press conference because our British Airways flight from London to Dublin was late,' says Colin Hart, boxing correspondent of the *Sun*. 'As soon as we arrive, we jump in a car and go to the hotel. We run in there and we meet Angelo and Chris Dundee, and a few other people but, of course, there's no Ali. No sign of Ali. We knew Angelo quite well at that stage, so we asked him: "Where's Ali?" "He's gone to bed," he says. "He's going to be in bed all day." Well, we had early editions to catch and Angelo could see we were quite perturbed, so he says: "What's the matter, fellas?" We told him our dilemma, and Angelo says: "Well, go and wake him up!" Can you imagine a trainer saying that to you today? We went to his room, hammered on the door, woke him up and he spoke to us for two and a half hours. We could have written a book with the stuff he gave us. He was sharing a room with his brother and, lying there on the bed, he decided to tell us how much it was costing him to keep Belinda and his family, he just went right through the family budget. At one stage we had to ask him to slow down to make sure we were getting all this down. There'll never be another man like him as long as the world is turning on its axis.'

At this remove, the quotes represent an opportunity to grasp Ali's ongoing struggle to balance his finances during this period of his life, and may at least partly explain why he ended up fighting six times between 1 April and 21 November that year, earning an estimated $1,610,000 for doing so. In the twenty-one months between defeating Ali at Madison Square Garden and losing to George Foreman in Jamaica, Frazier fought just twice.

'I was going through my cheque stubs with my wife the other day and found I had paid out $300,000 in the last six months," Ali told the English reporters. 'I bought a green Rolls-Royce hardtop to go with my silver Rolls-Royce convertible, and don't forget I have three other cars to keep going. Then there was the new swimming pool, the high wall around my house, my gold watch, and the training camp I am building for myself is costing me $80,000.'

He also announced that he was wearing a watch worth a mere $12, and that he would no longer be splurging on $200 suits. This new spirit of fiscal rectitude was one obvious by-product of his experience since losing to Frazier. His fights were not quite events of the magnitude they once had been. Promoters were having difficulty financing his bouts, to the extent that the second Quarry fight came under the microscope of the FBI. Acting on a tip-off, the bureau investigated erroneous claims that California Costa Nostra boss Nick Licata and the head of the New Orleans Mafia Carlos Marcello had been involved in bankrolling the fight. In this climate, Ali himself was learning the value of money.

'This watch tells the same time as the gold one and I will still look the greatest in $75 suits. I'm saving $100,000 dollars from this fight, money I can't touch for ten years. Before I meet Frazier, I will have $700,000 salted away. After Frazier, it will be a million and when I have two million, in maybe a couple of years, I'll be ready to retire. After this fight and the one with Floyd Patterson, in New York in September, I'm going to South Africa. They made me the offer and I have agreed, provided the audience is fifty-fifty, white and black. I want them to see what a black man can do. Pity they won't let me go in with their white champion.'

After allowing the journalists an eye-opening view of his

accounts, Ali gave them an obligatory line about his own legend.

'They tell me the air trip was rough but I slept most of the way. I used to hate flying but now I know God didn't intend me to go like that. He has something important for me to do.'

Elsewhere in the city that afternoon, Harold Conrad and Butty Sugrue were busy with important work at 'The Big Fight HQ', an office which had been rented at 21 Upper O'Connell Street. Its location on the main drag, within walking distance of Croke Park, the venue for the bout, made it convenient for all involved. The big arrival was splashed on the front page of the late editions of the *Evening Herald* – a photograph showed Ali poised to strike with his shillelagh, and a headline declared MUHAMMAD ALI COMES TO TOWN. If getting him to town was a triumph in itself, the co-promoters hoped the brouhaha surrounding Ali's entrance might give the advance ticket sales a much-needed boost.

That night, Conrad repaired to an enormous suite on the top floor of the Gresham Hotel on O'Connell Street. Passing up Opperman's and the added proximity to Ali it offered, he chose the Gresham to be near the office and right at the hub of activity. Conrad lived for the social occasions surrounding every fight, and already he envisaged the Gresham as the place where the journalists, ex-fighters and celebrities who are inevitably drawn towards the glamour of boxing would gather during the build-up. Not quite one hundred yards away, Sugrue was staying in a little flat around the corner on Sean McDermott Street. Some say he was renting it. Others that he was borrowing it from a friend. In any case, his choice offers an insight into his character.

'That was an example of the way Butty worked,' says Thomas Myler, then boxing correspondent of the *Evening Herald*. 'Whereas everyone else who was anybody was in the Gresham, he didn't want to stay in a swanky hotel. He could have afforded any hotel in town but the old country boy came out in him. You know the old story, you can take the boy out of the country but you can't take the country out of the boy. He was a small-time guy who came from modest beginnings. There were no airs and graces about him and he had no time for the toffs. He just wanted to put on the fight and let the people he was employing do the work. At the end of the day then, he wanted to head back to his flat on his own.'

The different lodgings they chose were indicative of what a very odd pair of co-promoters Sugrue and Conrad made.

When Harold met Butty

On the morning of 4 April 1972, Harold Conrad arrived in London from New York. Booking into his hotel, he was surprised to discover three messages from a man he had never met. Some guy by the name of Butty Sugrue sounded real anxious for him to get in touch. A former sports writer, Conrad had carved out a reputation as one of the slickest promoters and publicists in the American fight game. His curiosity pricked, he picked up the phone and rang the local number he'd been given. First thing he heard was a thick Irish accent launching into an elaborate tale about how he'd once spent some time with the great Joe Louis and was now in a position to make Conrad a rich man.

Always intrigued by the possibility of making money, Conrad took a cab to Shepherd's Bush where Sugrue and his wife Joan ran the Wellington, a sprawling Irish bar. After the preliminary introductions, Sugrue cut to the chase with his visitor.

'Could you get Muhammad Ali for a fight in Dublin?'

'Against whom?' asks Conrad.

'I'll leave that up to you.'

Conrad got this sort of thing all the time. Every city he passed through, there was a dreamer or a schemer who fancied bringing the greatest show in sport to his home town. Many knew of his credentials in advance and had prepared their pitch; others perked up immediately when they realised this was the guy who organised the famous photo shoot between a young Cassius Clay and the Beatles in Miami before the first bout with Sonny Liston in 1964. The man who persuaded Malcolm X to leave town for a few days so that ticket sales for that very fight wouldn't be affected by adverse publicity surrounding the

Nation of Islam. In boxing parlance, Conrad was a true heavyweight. His name was on very few posters but around the gyms there weren't many who could match his credentials.

The latest in a long line of people with an eye for the main chance, Sugrue had obviously done his homework and knew Conrad was the kind of person who could actually deliver Ali. Being polite, his visitor spun him a standard line about anything being possible once the money was right, and Sugrue, in innocence or mischief, thought he had a deal and stuck out his hand.

'We got a deal, let's shake.'

Not so fast. Tired of wasting time on chancers with neither the will nor the wealth to finance an Ali fight, Conrad decided to dampen this guy's ardour, telling him that there'd be no handshake until the publican could prove he had the wherewithal to come up with the cash. Sugrue didn't blink.

'No problem at all, not at all. How much will it take?'

'Three hundred thousand dollars,' replied Conrad, knowing full well that Ali was averaging in the region of $250,000 a fight just then.

'That's nothing at all, not at all,' he says. 'Come with me.'

They walked to a nearby branch of the Williams & Glyn Bank where, according to Conrad's recollection of events, the following dialogue took place inside the manager's office.

'Would you tell this man I'm good for $300,000,' asked Sugrue of the bank official.

'Yes, Butty Sugrue is good for $300,000,' he replied. 'This bank stands behind him.'

Freshly invigorated by that ringing endorsement, Sugrue couldn't resist enhancing his own position still further.

'And there's plenty more where that comes from,' he said.

Conrad was impressed. Sugrue had answered every question, passed every one of the initial tests designed to expose the fantasists and spare himself undue bother. Even when he outlined his terms for the deal, ridiculously one-sided as they were, his would-be collaborator appeared unmoved by the stringent conditions. Sugrue was to cover the expenses of bringing the entire Ali circus to town and, for delivering the fighter to Ireland, Conrad demanded a 50 per cent share of the profits without putting up a single penny himself. Only a man in Conrad's position could negotiate such favourable terms. It wasn't everybody who could confidently claim that persuading Ali to travel three thousand miles to a country he'd never visited before was well within his remit.

Of course, moments after Conrad warned him to make sure he had the letters of credit in order to guarantee the purses, Sugrue wasn't even thinking of the financial risks involved. After all, how could they possibly fail to make money? Radio and television ensured Ali had enjoyed massive popularity in Ireland since the early sixties and the opportunity to see him in the flesh would surely be an easy sell.

'You'll be thanking the day you met me,' Sugrue assured his co-promoter. 'We'll sell out every seat we put up in Dublin.'

Three days before Conrad's encounter with the bold Sugrue, Muhammad Ali climbed into the ring at Tokyo's Budokan Hall, wearing a lavishly embroidered silk kimono and carrying a sign predicting he would end his contest with Mac Foster in the fifth round. After subsequently watching him secure a unanimous decision at the end of a lacklustre fifteen, many in the audience thought the fight a bad April Fool's joke. Never in any danger of losing, Ali seemed to become bored and disinterested once Foster refused to go down in the face of prolonged early barrages. More than a year had passed since his defeat by Joe Frazier in Madison Square Garden on 8 March 1971, and the former champion had entered a curious phase in his career. No longer in forced exile but no longer the king.

Before beginning his post-Frazier rehabilitation against Jimmy Ellis at the Houston Astrodome on 26 July, he had come within a whisker of signing on for a bout with the basketball legend Wilt Chamberlain. When he learned of the public's indifference ahead of his next outing – Buster Mathis at the same venue four months later – he seriously suggested to one of the promoters that a fake kidnapping of him might work wonders at the box office. Not quite six weeks after that, just three American sports writers travelled to Zurich to watch him earn a facile victory over Blin, the German ex-butcher whose former profession didn't quite match his fighting style. By that stage, Frazier still hadn't returned to the ring, but Ali was having to go a little off Broadway in search of a crowd. Maybe *Sports Illustrated* had been right when the headline on its cover story after the epic in the Garden declared: END OF THE ALI LEGEND.

'The whole time I wasn't allowed to fight, no matter what the authorities said, it felt like I was the heavyweight champion of the world,' said Ali later. 'Then I lost to Joe Frazier. And what hurt most wasn't the money that losing cost me. It wasn't the punches I took. It was knowing that my title had gone. When I beat Sonny Liston I was too young to appreciate what I'd won. But when I lost to Frazier, I would have done anything except go against the will of Allah to get my title back.'

Following the defeat of Blin, Ali began 1972 by making a hajj to Mecca, the pilgrimage every Muslim is required to undertake at least once in their life. During that trip, he accompanied his manager Herbert Muhammad on Nation of Islam business in Tripoli. A $3 million loan that Libya had earlier agreed to make to the Nation had been slow in materialising, and Herbert correctly deduced that bringing Colonel Mu'ammar Gaddafi's favourite fighter to visit him might speed up the process. While preparing for their audience with the Libyan leader, Ali spent time joshing with Idi Amin, dictator of Uganda and, as he liked to boast, holder of that country's heavyweight title since 1951. The money finally came through and went towards making Muhammad's Mosque of Islam one of the ten largest religious complexes in America.

On a personal level, Ali had a mixed start to the year. His wife Belinda was pregnant with his first son, Muhammad Junior, who would be born on 14 May; one of his regular girlfriends Patricia Harvell was also carrying a child for him; and on 2 March, his first wife Sonjii won a court judgement for close on $50,000 in unpaid alimony. Ali wasn't in any serious financial trouble but he needed regular money coming in to fund his outgoings. There had been too many idle years. Over the course of his last four fights, the purses had decreased each time from a high of $450,000 against Ellis to a low of $200,000 for waltzing with Foster in Japan. Hardly chicken feed, it was nevertheless a far cry from the $2,500,000 he had earned losing to Frazier, and despite constant speculation about a rematch of mind-blowing financial dimensions, the new champion didn't look in any hurry to put his title on the line.

Few people would have known the lie of the land around Ali at that time better than Conrad. He had lost good money co-promoting the Blin farce, and the moment Sugrue sowed the seed in his brain, he envisaged Dublin as an opportunity to recoup his investment. Casting around for a likely opponent, he realised that after the criticism heaped on Ali for under-performing in Tokyo, and meeting a genuine contender for bum-of-the-month status in Zurich, a fighter with some vestige of credibility was essential to the success of the promotion.

Conrad called a friend of his in Cleveland, Ohio. A promoter-cum-manager-cum-matchmaker, Don Elbaum would later go down in boxing history as the person who introduced Don King to the sport. Back then, he owned 15 per cent of a Detroit heavyweight called Al 'Blue' Lewis. With nineteen knock outs and only four losses from thirty-four starts, Lewis was a good puncher who found it hard to get regular fights. Nobody on the way up wanted to take a chance in incurring a blemish on their record and those already at the top couldn't be paid large enough purses to outweigh the risk of him knocking them out. As a consequence, Lewis struggled to find opponents, and in the whole of 1971, he'd fought only twice.

'We started talking about candidates and I said immediately: "Jesus, it has to be Al 'Blue' Lewis,"' says Elbaum. 'I told Hal: "This is the perfect fight for him, he's a double tough guy, he's big, he's strong, he can punch and it could be a great fight because he'll stay in there with Ali."'

It only remained for Conrad to thrash out a deal with Herbert Muhammad. When the proposal of a fight in Dublin was first put to him, Ali's manager asked for $250,000 for his fighter. From there, the negotiations continued downwards. Conrad pleaded poverty on behalf of 'the poor people in Ireland', arguing that a high fee would preclude the ordinary worker from attending the event. He then played his trump card, reminding Herbert Muhammad that it was he and he alone who got bilked on the financially disastrous Blin fight. Eventually, they agreed that $200,000 was a fair amount.

Throughout their discussion, one unspoken factor influenced the way they did business. Conrad was owed a serious favour. He wasn't a Muslim. He wasn't a black. Yet few people in Ali's inner circle enjoyed the standing he did. When it mattered most, he'd proved his mettle. After Ali lost his licence for refusing induction into the US Army in April 1967, nobody worked harder to get him back in the ring than Conrad. Nobody. Sure, his motivation throughout those three and a half fallow years was professional more than personal; the longer the champ was down and out, the more Conrad knew that the first fight back would be as big as they come. To this end, he criss-crossed America and beyond in search of a venue, a town, a politician who shared his view that this event – the one destined for a special place in history – was the one to be involved with.

'Conrad's finest hour may have been his effort on behalf of Muhammad Ali, when the controversial champion was dethroned and driven into fistic exile for his opposition to the Vietnam War,' wrote Budd Schulberg. 'Conrad was neither an advocate of black power nor exactly a civil rights activist but he had been instrumental in getting the young Cassius the title shot against Liston and had become one of Clay/Ali's closest honky friends. He also knew there would be no serious money for the heavyweight title until the usurper, Joe Frazier, proved his right to that title in a shoot-out with Ali. We watched Conrad as he roamed the continent year after year in search of a ring for "The Fight of the Century".'

'He tried Canada, Baja California and states beyond the jurisdiction of the self-important bureaucrats who ran the commission. Every time he thought he had it made, someone threw a patriotic monkey wrench into Conrad's wheel. At last, he helped jawbone a fight in Georgia, of all places, against perennial white hope Jerry Quarry, something neither the Honourable Elijah Muhammad, Sidney Poitier, Bill Cosby, nor the Reverend Jesse Jackson had been able to do. Thanks to Conrad, who even helped set up the ring and personally arrange the chairs that wild night in Atlanta, Ali was on the road back to national acceptance as a world champion.'

Early in his professional life, Conrad was a boxing writer with the *Brooklyn Eagle*, and he and Buff Schulberg became good friends, knocking around the New York fight scene together. The Oscar-winning author of *On the Waterfront* based Humphrey Bogart's troubled publicist character in *The Harder They Fall* on his pal. Before evolving into one of the sport's most renowned players in the sixties and seventies, Conrad had dabbled in several different careers. Having served as an intelligence officer in the US army Air Corps during World War II, he worked in public relations in the casino business and moved in the *demimonde* of legendary forties gangsters like Lucky Luciano, Frank Costello and Bugsy Siegel. He wrote a dime novel called *The Battle at Apache Pass* which sold over a million copies and even did some screenwriting in Hollywood where his best-known work was *Sunny Side of the Street*.

Directing operations around the 1961 clash between Floyd Patterson and Ingemar Johansson in Miami, Conrad encountered a precocious nineteen-year-old Cassius Clay for the first time. Having subsequently handled both Patterson-Liston bouts, he played a vital role in keeping things running smoothly in the tumultuous build-up to Clay's attempt to dethrone Liston three years later. When news broke of Clay's impending embrace of the Nation of Islam – he had invited Malcolm X and his family to stay with him before the fight – the implications for the box office in Miami were huge. Unless Clay agreed to publicly disassociate himself from Islam, Bill McDonald, the promoter, was going to pull the plug.

Enter Conrad at his most brilliant and diplomatic in a role that would become one of the cornerstones of his legend. He struck a deal with McDonald. If he could persuade Malcolm X to leave town, the promotion would go ahead as planned. Arriving at the house where Clay was billeted, Conrad encountered a frosty reception from a host of Nation of Islam followers in suits and ties. Even Clay himself who had never been anything but amicable towards Conrad was now evincing a certain air of disdain.

Eventually, Conrad sat down with Malcolm X and convinced him that as the most well-known Muslim in America at the time and the one figure whom journalists in particular recognised, his continued presence in the city was actually going to cost Clay his shot at the title. After a period of reflection, Malcolm X agreed to fade from view but on his own terms.

'All right, I'll go,' he said, 'but I'm coming back for the fight.' When Conrad extended his hand to shake on it, Malcolm X's only response was to lightly touch his wrist.

Way more than a mere publicist or promoter, Conrad was a player, a spin doctor long before that term came into vogue. Like so many others, Malcolm X discovered that this man's true talent was the ability to coax and cajole someone in a direction the person didn't necessarily want to go. He'd honed these unique skills over many years, schmoozing with mob heavies in Miami, walking the streets of Manhattan with Damon Runyon and hanging out in Havana with Ernest Hemingway during the revolution. Another of his masterful displays came in Lewiston, Maine, during the build-up to the rematch between Ali and Liston in May 1965, when he somehow turned a bit of harmless banter into a worldwide news story.

With the fight having been shuttled around from reluctant city to reluctant city before finally settling on remote Lewiston, Conrad was desperately seeking to drum up publicity to sell tickets in the theatres that were going to be showing the fight live on closed-circuit television. Meeting Jose Torres, the then world light-heavyweight champion in the Poland Spring Inn, Conrad joked that since the fighter was attending the bout to write a newspaper column, he would have to give him a ticket to sit with the working press. Torres feigned dismay at the very suggestion, pointing out that with the scurrilous rumours flying around about certain Muslims coming to kill Ali to avenge the assassination of Malcolm X three months earlier, he didn't want to be in the line of fire.

It was a throwaway line mocking the mood in the ranks of the press where every hour seemed to bring a new story about a mythical car full of Malcolm X's aggrieved acolytes being spotted on the road from New York to Lewiston. Except Torres's gag caught the ear of Jimmy Cannon, the celebrated newspaper columnist. Catching the fever that was going around town, Cannon told Conrad that Torres's reluctance to sit near the ring was surely further evidence that something bad was about to go down. Conrad listened to these fresh concerns and with the alchemist's eye for mixing materials to good effect, grabbed Cannon by the arm and, with all the fake sincerity he could muster, begged: 'Jimmy, please do me a favour, don't print that story!'

The perfect double-bluff, Conrad knew that an old-school reporter of Cannon's ilk could not possibly keep that to himself. Next morning, every Hearst newspaper in America led the front page with a Jimmy Cannon exclusive about the forthcoming murder of Ali. The police then reacted to the headlines by asking Conrad whether they should think about beefing up security by searching all spectators for weapons as they arrive at the fight. No sooner did Conrad assure the police chief that this new precaution was an excellent idea than he fed the story to a reporter and spawned another day's worth of front-page news. Over the previous eighteen months, America had witnessed the assassination of President John F. Kennedy and the subsequent shooting of his alleged killer, Lee Harvey Oswald, on television, and Conrad wasn't averse to capitalising on the contemporary paranoia.

Conrad was married to Mara Lynn, a professional dancer he had met when reviewing a show of hers for the *New York Mirror* in 1948. As an actress, a featured role in the Marilyn Monroe vehicle *Let's Make Love* was the height of her cinematic achievements, but the pair of them together were one of the most glamorous couples around boxing. She was equally formidable in her own right. One New Year's Eve at PJ Clarke's in Manhattan, Jake La Motta discovered that much to his cost. When he tried to perform one of his party tricks – instead of kissing somebody politely on the cheek, he would attempt to put his tongue in their mouth – she poured rum and Coke over his head and the bar erupted into applause.

Throughout heavyweight boxing's golden age, the party which Harold and Mara traditionally threw the night before a big fight was always the place to find the literary and journalistic giants at play. When Conrad published his memoir, *Dear Muffo* in 1982, and appropriately subtitled it '35 years in the Fast Lane', Schulberg contributed an introduction and Norman Mailer wrote the foreword.

The eloquent testimony of such men of letters counted for little enough when Conrad flew to Dublin on 17 April to announce the match had been made. The Irish boxing writers knew his name well and realised this tall, thin figure, with the dapper wardrobe and perfectly coiffured moustache, held serious sway in the sweet science. Still, it was quite a stretch for them to imagine this dandy with a line of patter straight out of *Guys and Dolls* could live up to the promise of bringing Ali to a city which hadn't seen a world-title fight in forty-nine years. Watching Conrad holding court in the company of Butty Sugrue, a man who had been involved in one or two dubious enterprises in his time, didn't exactly inspire confidence about the future prospects of seeing the former champion up close either.

At first glance, Conrad and Sugrue were a study in contrasts. The epitome of New York sophistication, urbane and literary, Conrad had once helped George Plimpton organise a meeting so that Ali could sit down to write a poem with Marianne Moore. Schooled in the ways of television, brazed by a stint swimming with sharks in Hollywood, he was already a legend in the world of public relations. By comparison, Sugrue was rural, uneducated, a classic graduate of the university of life whose only real tool was an uncanny ability to wring a few quid from the least promising circumstance. Yet they had much in common too, each was adept at turning any situation to their own advantage, capable of seeing and seizing an opportunity before others even recognised the chance was there. And when it came to knowing how to generate a headline or two, well, they both knew a thing or two about that.

'Sugrue was a Kerryman who nobody really took seriously, and he comes over to Dublin and he says he's going to promote a fight involving Muhammad Ali, the former world heavyweight champion,' says Thomas Myler, then boxing correspondent of the *Evening Herald*. 'People thought it was a joke. Professional boxing had been a dead sport in Dublin. The city was a graveyard for the sport and now, here was a man claiming he was going to bring over one of the greatest champions of all time. Everyone in the town says: "This will never happen." Even when he publicly announced it, journalists and members of the Irish Boxing Board of Control all said they seriously doubted whether it would go ahead.

'What happened, of course, is that he announced the fight and began publicising it but didn't even get prior permission from the Irish Boxing Board. I'm sure his intention was to start the ball rolling and hope then that they'd go along with it. I was very suspicious myself, very doubtful he'd be able to do it. At first, he didn't even announce the opponent, he just said he could get Ali. Then there was talk of Ali maybe fighting Jerry Quarry or Oscar Bonavena in Dublin and finally he announced Al "Blue" Lewis and none of us really thought too much about Al "Blue" Lewis.'

Used to having journalists eager to do his bidding, Conrad was dismayed by the attitude of the Irish media. If they weren't pooh-poohing the idea outright, they were making jokes about it. He had expected an enthusiastic press corps, anxious to get behind the promotion and give it a helpful push. After all, it was in their interests to be of assistance. What reporter didn't covet a week of Muhammad Ali on their patch, with the inevitable torrent of easy quotes that entailed. Instead, he found a sceptical bunch, their cynicism a result perhaps of them knowing far more about his co-promoter than he did.

A master at garnering cheap publicity, Sugrue had a reputation for often delivering less than he promised. Some reporters went as far as privately whispering in Conrad's ear that his new partner wasn't exactly the most reliable, and might pull out at the eleventh hour. Conrad's only reaction to this information was to assure them that contracts had been signed, letters of credit secured and believe it or believe it not, Ali would be fighting in Dublin on a bill put together as a joint venture with the much maligned Butty Sugrue.

Barely four years had passed since the Sugrue name had last been in the headlines. In his second attempt at one of the lesser spotted world records, he persuaded a barman at the Elephant's Head, a pub he owned in north London, to spend sixty-one days in a coffin, buried eleven feet below the surface. After Tipperary native Mike Meaney finally emerged from his subterranean resting place to a crowd including the glamorous figure of Diana Dors, Sugrue put him on the back of a lorry and, in the manner of successful sports teams, paraded him through the streets of Kilburn.

One of three brothers from Killorglin in south-west Kerry, Michael 'Butty' Sugrue had already packed a lot into his forty-eight years on earth. Variously described as somewhere between five foot five and five foot eight in height, with a few stubborn wisps of hair clinging to his otherwise rapidly balding head, he was a small, squat man blessed with incredible strength. As a young lad working the peat bogs in Offaly, he used to entertain his larger colleagues by hoisting them over his head and holding them there. In the pre-television era, that sort of gift was remarkable enough for him to parlay it into a modicum of fame.

Leaving the turf-cutting behind him, he spent much of the forties and early fifties traversing the country as a headline act with Duffy's Circus.

Most evenings, he'd enter the ring to the sound of his colleague Michael Doyle fingering the accordion, the audience gasping the instant they realised Doyle was actually perched atop a chair which Sugrue held between his teeth while walking along. The posters declared him 'Ireland's Strongest Man!' and few quibbled with the billing. Those that did were invited up into the spotlight to see if they could match his feats. Usually, he lifted four fifty-six-pound shop weights attached to a steel cart axle (also fifty-six pounds) above his head and then watched the dissenters fail one by one to replicate his action.

Another trick was to sit ten men on a trailer before dragging it around the big top with a rope clenched between his teeth. Typical sideshow fare, it was the kind of act that the people of a town remembered and it made Sugrue famous. When the men repaired to the pubs afterwards, they spent hours figuring out how such a small man could be so strong. At school the next day, kids would talk of little else. Over time, his reputation grew and grew to the extent that the story about him tugging a double-decker bus across O'Connell Bridge in Dublin with those ever-resilient gnashers became his calling card. Of course, it helped greatly that some of the more ludicrous yarns about him were actually true.

In August 1953, he returned to his home town for Puck Fair, Killorglin's annual three-day festival, where thousands congregate ostensibly to trade livestock but mostly to party. There, the clash between himself and Jack Doyle, the former heavyweight boxer turned actor and singer, topped the bill in a wrestling tournament the pair had organised themselves. That Doyle was a native of neighbouring County Cork added spice to the contest, but Sugrue was a far superior grappler and won out easily in two rounds. Later, he stripped down to his trousers for a local photographer and, bare-chested, wrestled King Puck, the wild mountain goat whose anointing as royalty was part of the

26

annual ritual at the festival. The enduring picture of Sugrue grimacing as he got to grips with the animal's forelegs was of little consolation to the other wrestlers; they spent much of that evening looking for Doyle, Sugrue and the money they were owed. Ireland is a small country and when somebody welches on a debt like that, however small, the story gets around.

Emigrating to London in the early sixties, Sugrue arrived in a city teeming with Irish and opportunity. A teetotaller, he got involved in the pub business, an industry where his name recognition and flair for promotion brought his compatriots flocking to his establishments. If his quiet manner and gentle ways belied his illustrious past as Ireland's strongest man, customers caught glimpses now and then of his abilities. Any troublemakers left the bar in a hurry. He wouldn't fight anybody, he'd just grab at them, and once he'd gained a substantial hold, the miscreant was lifted bodily from the premises and warned not to return. Celebrities were treated in a different fashion.

'Butty was supposed to be the strongest publican in captivity,' remembered Paddy Byrne, a Dubliner involved in boxing in London at the time. 'Part of the attraction was that he used to lift up celebrities on his chest. He had a special chair with a bar that sat across his chest. I saw him lift Henry Cooper up that way one time. The guy had an enormous chest, he was a real pocket battleship.'

In 1964, Cooper was centrally involved in Sugrue's first attempt at making serious money from boxing. He put together a variety show to tour Ireland, with Cooper and the ubiquitous Jack Doyle the key ingredients in the evening of vaudevillian entertainment. After being warmed up by Irish dancers and showgirls, Doyle, an excellent tenor, would sing a few songs, and Cooper would then fight in an exhibition against his brother Jim. Quite a package, the show opened well at Dublin's Mansion House but faltered as soon as it moved out into the country and they quickly cut their losses. The failure hardly mattered to Cooper: his manager had insisted his client be paid in advance.

Not long after Lord Nelson's Pillar was blown up in

O'Connell Street in Dublin in 1966, word swept around the Irish community in London that the head of the statue would be making an appearance in the Elephant's Head on a certain night. The place was packed to the rafters when the proprietor announced that unfortunately some ne'er-do-wells had stolen the head from a wheelbarrow in the backyard the previous evening. Only Sugrue could get away with disappointing people on that scale. In time, the story developed legs and tails, and in one of the later versions, the admiral's head had indeed been placed on the bar where it was abused by the customers. For all the tall tales and half-truths, Sugrue's friends regarded him as intensely loyal, and he had an admirable history of assisting Irish people in London.

'My impression of him was of a fella who would do anything he could to help you out,' says John McCormack, a Dubliner who held the British light-heavyweight title from 1967 to 1969. 'For instance, I went into the Elephant's Head one night to try to sell a few tickets for a fight I had coming up. The minute I walked in and met Butty, he said: "Right, John, get up on the stage there." Margaret Barry, an ould tinker woman who used to play the banjo, a gruff, black-headed woman, was already up on the stage. And Jack Doyle beside her. Jack used to sing three songs every night for fifteen pounds. Anyway, I go up and take the microphone to tell the crowd when I'm fighting and who I'm fighting, trying to flog a few seats. Then the crowd started to ask me questions and while this is going on, Butty is selling tickets for my fight from behind the bar. Of course then Jack leans over and says to me: "Listen, I sing three songs here for fifteen pound and the way the time is going now, I'm down to two with your talking, so would you do me a favour and get down 'cause you're costing me a fiver already!" At that time now, fifteen pound was half a week's wages, but Doyle was down on his luck, and rather than give it to him into his hand and demean him further, Butty used to get him to sing these beautiful, old come-all-ye's for it. That was a typical scene in the pub and that was the kind of thing he'd do for a fella.'

Sugrue's benevolence towards his friend Doyle, an increasingly pathetic alcoholic as time wore on, was more than financial. If Doyle needed a place to stay, he knew his Kerry friend would always come through for him. What Sugrue got from the friendship was an entrée into a more glamorous world. Once, he accompanied his pal to Elstree Studios where Doyle met Marlon Brando on the set of *The Countess of Hong Kong*. Both men had been married to Movita, a Mexican film star, and Brando wanted information from Doyle that would help him negotiate the terms of his divorce. Reportedly, Sugrue was asked along as security in case the discussion between the ex-husband and the wannabe ex-husband turned ugly.

'Butty really did have incredible strength,' says John McCormack's brother Pat, a welterweight also based in London in the late sixties and early seventies. 'I ended up taking part in a publicity stunt for the Ali fight and I still have the photograph somewhere. Butty lifted myself and Paddy Maguire, a bantamweight from Belfast, clean up off the floor for the photographers. He literally picked us up one in each hand inside the pub. For a fellow of his size and at that stage in his life, it was an incredible achievement. We weren't heavyweights but there was eighteen or nineteen stones there between the two of us.'

Despite his low standing with the Irish sports writers, Sugrue had succeeded in bringing Joe Louis on a tour of the country in 1967 and, buoyed by this enterprise, he saw nothing to dissuade him from the notion that he could also deliver Ali. In his experience, once the money could be found, anything was possible and it was in this spirit he had tracked down Conrad and got the process underway. For all his background in strength-based gimmickry and travelling fairs, he had proved a shrewd enough businessman. The Elephant's Head in Kilburn and the Wellington on Shepherd's Bush Green were enormous pubs and thriving concerns in his hands, a point proven by the way his bank rowed in behind the Ali project from the start.

Even though it sometimes suited him to pretend differently, Sugrue was neither a country bumpkin nor a carnival barker.

Those reporters who cocked a snook at his aspirations and took it upon themselves to warn Conrad off simply couldn't believe the claim that the short, stocky Kerryman in their midst had already deposited $25,000 in a New York bank as a guarantee that on 19 July, at Croke Park, the headquarters of the Gaelic Athletic Association (GAA) in Dublin, Muhammad Ali was set to be the headline act. The doubting Thomases would only have to wait three months to put their hands in the wounds.

3

Monaghan's Labour of Love

A few weeks before his grand entrance at Dublin airport, as those around him were making the usual arrangements for any trip to Europe, Muhammad Ali found time to make a call to England. When Paddy Monaghan picked up the phone at his home in Abingdon, outside Oxford, he found his old friend in particularly good form. From the off, he was on the offensive.

'I'm fightin' in Ireland, the land of your ancestors, Paddy,' said Ali.

'Hang on a minute, me old sunshine,' replied Monaghan. 'Ireland is my country.'

'Naw, it ain't.'

'Yes, it is!'

'Look, Paddy, where you been living all your life?'

'Here in Abingdon.'

'Right. So your home country is England.'

'No, it isn't!'

'Yeah, it is.'

They continued in this pantomime fashion until Ali couldn't suppress his chuckling any longer. When Paddy was five, the Monaghan family had departed Ederney, County Fermanagh, and taken the cattle boat to England in search of a better life. The new surroundings soon thieved Ulster from his accent, but he clung passionately to his Irishness. Ali knew him well enough to realise that nothing vexed him more than to question that part of his identity.

'Who are you fighting?' asked Monaghan, after the sparring had stopped.

'Joe Frazier,' answered Ali.

'Ah, come on, Muhammad. Stop taking the piss!'

'What does that mean?'

'It means you're winding me up, that's what.'

'What's that mean? Am I talking to a clock?'

'It means you're bullshitting me!'

'All right, Paddy, the fight's against Al "Blue" Lewis.'

With that, Ali made clear the real purpose of his call. He wanted Monaghan in Dublin for the week beforehand, and in his corner as a second for the bout itself. To understand why he wished to bestow that unique honour on an unemployed hod carrier from Oxfordshire, it is necessary to go back to 1967 when Ali was stripped of his title on account of his refusal to be inducted into the US Army. Seeing his idol lose his crown outside the ring had greatly angered Monaghan. To him, Ali had been more than just another fighter to watch and appreciate from afar. He'd been an inspiration in the most curious way.

'I left school knowing far more about how to use a shovel than a pen,' says Monaghan. 'I'd been a fan of his from the 1960 Olympics but whenever I saw a newspaper with his photo in it, I'd have to take it, put it under my arm and head home to my mother. She'd have to read the report to me because I was illiterate. At work on the building sites, blokes would be reading the paper and say: "There's a photo of Ali here, Paddy." I'd take the paper and pretend to be reading it because I was ashamed that I couldn't actually understand what it said. You have to understand that Ali was my college of knowledge. Unbeknown to him, I learned to read and write through him and that's why I stood up for him in 1967. You didn't have to be a brain surgeon to work out that what the boxing authorities were doing to him was wrong, and I suppose growing up Irish in England, I felt a natural sense of injustice too.'

Watching footage of the then Cassius Clay defeating Alejandre Lavorante one afternoon in the summer of 1962, it struck Monaghan that his mother wasn't always going to be around to assist him in his obsession with the American boxer. He decided it was about time that he learned for himself. Having mastered the alphabet, he plotted a path through the works of

Beatrix Potter before graduating to the Enid Blyton canon. For somebody approaching twenty that was quite a journey to take, and fortunately the progression of Clay's career served constantly to remind him why he needed to be able to read and write.

In June 1963, Monaghan took a day off work and caught the train to London to see Clay training in preparation for this first encounter with Henry Cooper. He arrived late at the TA Centre in Shepherd's Bush and found a crowd waiting at the door for Clay to leave. Watching the twenty-one-year-old interact with the people reinforced Monaghan's view that he was a different sort of sportsman. On his way out, Clay stopped and appeared to mistake Monaghan for somebody he knew. So overawed was he by this close encounter that he forgot to ask for an autograph. Monaghan returned to Abingdon, approached his studies with renewed fervour and always felt that the desire to keep up with his favourite boxer's progress was central to him becoming literate. Seeing his hero slighted in this way four years later, he decided to repay the favour by taking up the cudgels on behalf of the deposed champion.

A campaign to gather enough signatures to force the boxing authorities to rethink their actions started with him going door to door on the estate where he lived, badgering his neighbours to put pen to paper. From there, he moved on to his workmates at the MG car factory, and before he'd finished he had gathered 22,224 names and addresses of people willing to share his view that 'Ali is our Champ!' Eventually, Monaghan started describing Ali as 'The People's Champ', an even catchier moniker when tilting at windmills in such grand style. He travelled to London numerous times, walking and up down Park Lane with a placard publicising his cause, regularly performing at Speakers' Corner, and on one occasion, he handed a letter marked 'For the urgent and personal attention of the President' into the US Embassy in Grosvenor Square.

As the movement gained momentum, letters of support arrived from as far away as Australia and China. The odd nasty missive came his way too and at one point he drew the opprobrium of the Ku Klux Klan who wrote to him from a town in Georgia and labelled him 'a nigger-lovin' son of a bitch'. He returned their letter with the rejoinder 'Fuck Off' and they never wrote back. The petitioning evolved over time into the Muhammad Ali fan club with Monaghan so identifiable as its founder that very often his postman delivered letters addressed simply to 'Paddy Monaghan, Muhammad Ali fan club, England'.

After Ali returned from exile, Monaghan lost none of his defiance. On 14 June 1971, the day that Joe Frazier flew into Heathrow as undisputed heavyweight champion, he had an unexpected welcome party. Bearing his ubiquitous 'Ali is our Champ!' placard, Monaghan had come to face down Frazier and informed him: "Welcome to England. When you get back to America tell Howard Hughes, Edgar Hoover and Nixon that you're just their champ – and that Muhammad Ali is the people's champion."

'The fury in Frazier's eyes was frightening,' wrote Monaghan in his memoir *The Sunshine in My Life.* 'Through gritted teeth, he snarled: "Put that fucking thing down!" "Nope – and fuck you too." Then he bent forward, his forehead against mine, and repeated: "Put it down, you bastard, I'm gonna nail you if you don't." '

After airport police and the members of Frazier's pop group, the Knock Outs, had pulled the two men apart, a brief melee ensued. One of the backing singers aimed a sly kick at Monaghan, and he reacted with his fists flying. Before the police could intervene again and spirit him away from the by now livid Frazier entourage, he had suffered a fat lip and a few cuts and bruises. Even when being escorted to safety, he shouted after his opponents: 'You lot ain't knock outs, you're a bunch of fucking drop-outs!' If the rhyming scheme wasn't quite Ali material, Monaghan's lone stand was enough to earn him a mention on the ITN news that night.

It also merited a severe telling-off from his wife Sandra. Two years earlier, Monaghan had been diagnosed as epileptic and ordered by his doctor to cut back on his pro-Ali activities. That condition also cost him his job at the car factory and forced him to return to his past in order to keep money coming into the house. As a teenage tearaway, he had often participated in bare-knuckle bouts for some quick cash. Upon meeting Sandra, he'd left that world behind him. After being medically disqualified from hod-carrying or factory work, the bare-knuckle arena represented one way of earning regular money. An illegal and, for an epileptic, potentially fatal chance to make a few bob, it was nevertheless the path he chose.

'I didn't like bare-knuckle fighting but it was something I had to do. I had to provide for my family somehow. I hated going out to isolated barns in the countryside, I hated the sound of bones hitting bones and all the blood. It was a savage thing to have to do but I did it. No one forced me into those fights. I knew what to expect and I know how to dish it out myself. The fights lasted no more than three three-minute rounds and the rules were simple. No gouging, no punching at the throat, no kicking, no punching below the belt and no biting. When I saw a few fighters who were missing an ear or a piece of an ear, I realised that not everybody obeyed the rules.

'Eventually, I had to give it up. I came back one Sunday evening covered in blood. My eyes were swollen shut, my ribs were broken and the front of my nose was ripped after being bitten by the dirty bastard I was fighting. On the way home, one of my pals had stopped the bleeding from my eyes using old tea leaves, and axle grease and Vaseline. Sandra collapsed to the ground when she saw the state of me but the reaction of the kids was worse. I stuck my head in to say hello to them and they screamed, they thought I was a bloody monster. That night, I promised Sandra I'd stop. The thought that I scared my wife and kids that much hurt more than any fight I'd ever been in.'

His tour of duty on that circuit left Monaghan with lingering bite marks on either nostril, still visible scars of old cuts around his eyes, and with the knuckles on both hands almost ground away to nothing. Throughout that Hemingwayesque chapter in his life, his passion for the Ali cause remained constant. When he read that Herbert Muhammad was making a trip to London, he travelled up to the Royal Lancaster Hotel to show him a sack of the fan mail he'd received for Muhammad's client. Taken aback by this, Ali's manager flicked through a sample and asked Monaghan to write down his name and address for him. A few weeks later, a letter arrived bearing a Philadelphia postmark. It read:

Memo from Muhammad Ali

Dear Paddy
   Keep up the good work. I will see you when I'm in England,
Good luck,
Muhammad Ali.

That brief note and the recognition it implied made all his campaigning seem worthwhile. Better was to follow. In October 1971, Ovaltine brought Ali to London on a promotional tour and Monaghan was at Heathrow airport for the arrival. He'd carried with him a bag full of correspondence from fans and a strip of red carpet. Hoping to get close enough to hand over the letters, roll out the shag pile and shake Ali's hand, he got more than he bargained for. When Ali finally emerged from behind the security barrier, Monaghan put the carpet on the ground and introduced himself.

'So you're Paddy Monaghan,' said Ali. 'I been hearing your name a lot back home, hearing about the good work you've been doing.'

From there, the day turned into a magic-carpet ride. Ali invited him aboard his Rolls-Royce for the journey into the city centre, and insisted they eat together in a suite at the Royale Lancaster. Wearing second-hand clothes, Monaghan felt ill at ease in the salubrious surroundings, and when Ali asked him what he did for a living, he found himself lying. Not wanting to be seen as just another hanger-on looking to freeload, he spun a yarn about making cars. Still, he must have made quite an impression. At the end of his visit, Ali gave Monaghan his number and asked him to ring in a few weeks to make arrangements to go see him in America.

On 17 February 1972, Monaghan travelled on a plane for the first time. Before he left, his brother Seamus loaned him two shirts and a pair of shoes and warned him that when the Americans saw him walking along with Ali, they'd be saying: 'Here's the champ, what's he doing with the tramp?' During the flight, he made the mistake of informing the couple sitting beside him that Ali had paid for his ticket. They couldn't stop sniggering for the duration. At the other end, he was met by a chauffeur-driven limo that took him to Cherry Hill, New Jersey. Ali was away in Pittsburgh but Belinda cooked him a meal before driving him to his hotel nearby. Next morning, his host came calling.

'Within three weeks, we jetted off to many places, and we grew to like each other more,' wrote Monaghan. 'Here was I in the United States as a guest of Muhammad Ali, travelling with him every day and being privileged to work with him as his cornerman during exhibition bouts; and meeting all these celebrities: film stars, pop stars, sports stars, staying in posh hotels and being driven in posh cars. Privilege followed privilege.'

At Jackie Gleason's birthday party, Monaghan sat between Ali and Mickey Rooney. Around about the time dessert was being served, Rooney turned to him, saying: 'Welcome to Millionaires Unanimous, now what line are you in yourself?' Monaghan's reply was quick: 'I'm not in any line at the moment, in fact, the last line I was in was the dole line. I'm an unemployed builder's labourer.' Rooney dissolved into laughter, thinking this a suitably funny riposte, and left it at that.

Later in the evening, Rooney approached Monaghan again, this time with a more serious bent. In the interim, Ali had mischievously informed Rooney that Monaghan was a top

London stockbroker who'd just flown in to keep Ali abreast of the latest market movements. That news really got Rooney's dander up and he was practically begging. 'Come on, Paddy, give me a bit of the action and I'll cut you a percentage,' he pleaded, pressing his card into Monaghan's hand. In vain, Monaghan tried to point out that everything he had on that night was borrowed and even his haircut had been a going-away present from his mother, but Rooney just wouldn't listen.

And Monaghan was telling the truth. He had very little. Returning from his sojourn in America, one of his first tasks involved ringing Ali to ask him to send a letter attesting that he funded the entire trip. During his weeks away, the Department of Health and Social Security had cut off his invalidity benefit, arguing that if a man unable to work could jet off across the Atlantic, he hardly required their services. Armed with a two-page cable from Ali, Monaghan caught the bus into Oxford to see if that would be enough evidence for the DHSS, and one of the inspectors ended up asking him for the cable as a souvenir. He refused.

Just three months after his spell mixing with the glitterati in America, the invitation to meet Ali in Dublin left him with one slight problem – the price of getting from Oxford to Ireland. Knowing his accommodation would be looked after by the camp, he figured the only way he could rustle up the air fare was to sell a signed painting of Rocky Marciano. Fortunately, it didn't come to that. He did a deal with an enterprising travel agency anxious enough to get its hands on the names and addresses of the fan club. They paid for his return ticket and a hotel room until such time as he linked up with the Ali party.

At Dublin airport, Ali made a point of introducing Monaghan at the press conference as his biggest fan. Insisting that his closest Irish friend travel with him in his car to Opperman's, the two were very rarely apart for the rest of the week. Monaghan sat in on more than one interview, informing journalists that he was the only member of the entourage supporting a wife and three kids with £17 per week dole money. Ali's offer to allow him to work the corner during the fight, though, was to unwittingly precipitate a crisis and, for a time, put the bout itself in serious doubt.

It began when an official from the Irish Boxing Board of Control turned up at the hotel to sort out a few minor details regarding the contest. Just as a matter of course he asked whether there would be anybody apart from Angelo Dundee working his corner. Ali informed him that Paddy Monaghan was to be his second and the official asked to see Monaghan's second's licence. Monaghan confessed that he didn't have one and the official's countenance changed for the worse. Citing board regulations, he informed the two men that no unlicenced second could be allowed to work the fight.

Ali's response to this was typically stubborn. 'Paddy don't need no licence 'cause he's my friend!' said Ali pointedly, 'he's going to be in my corner, you can tell that to your board.'

This was the sort of imbroglio where Harold Conrad invariably showed his mettle. Experienced in the ways of bureaucratic officials the world over, and knowing how defiant Ali could be on the most trivial matters, he went straight to Monaghan. Appealing to his good nature, he asked him to go to Ali and tell him that he no longer wanted to work the corner, the kerfuffle surrounding his lack of a licence having taken the gloss off the idea. Much to Conrad's dismay, Monaghan wasn't for turning. He tried another tack.

Those years hanging with mobsters on the casino scene had taught Conrad a valuable lesson in life. Everybody had a price. The trick lay in discovering how much it was. Knowing Monaghan's financial situation, the promoter figured this little wrinkle in proceedings could be easily ironed out with a cheque. Surely, if Monaghan was, as he so publicly claimed, an unemployed builder's labourer, he'd come cheap enough. Imagine his dismay when Monaghan told him that no money would persuade him to lie to Ali. In good faith, his friend had offered him the thrill of a lifetime. No matter how broke he was, Monaghan couldn't renege on that for money. Conrad departed their private meeting, muttering something about loyalty and buying off the Board of Control.

Even if it never did come to that, the brinksmanship wasn't over yet. A subsequent meeting between the board, the promoters, Monaghan and Ali in his suite yielded no progress. At one point in that heated discussion, Monaghan offered to pull out and a resolution appeared to have been reached. Step forward Ali to showcase his famous obstinacy and reiterate his stance. He wanted to reward one of his most loyal subjects with this unique gift and officials were not going to stop him from doing so. His contribution ended the debate. Out in the corridor, however, Dundee could be heard explaining to the board that his fighter wasn't one for backing down, and if he got irritated enough, might walk out on the promotion altogether.

Next morning, a courier arrived at the hotel with a second's licence, issued to one Patrick Monaghan, c/o Muhammad Ali, Opperman's Hotel. In four separate inscriptions on the document, somebody from the board wrote 'For the 19 July Show Only'. It was as if the official wanted to remind all involved how much they had bent their rules to accommodate this request. That Ali was willing to flex his muscles on behalf of Monaghan showed how close the two had become, and when he expressed an interest in skipping his road work early one morning and using the time to get a view of Dublin before the city woke up, there was only one person he wanted as his tour guide.

At 5 a.m., they drove into town from Opperman's, passing the journey with Monaghan imparting what he knew about the 1916 Easter Rising and in particular recounting the storied role the General Post Office on O'Connell Street played in the rebellion. After an Irish Republic had been declared from the steps of the GPO, the volunteers stationed there came under heavy fire from an English gunboat that had travelled up the River Liffey, and although the building was gutted during subsequent fighting, the impressive Doric portico that jutted out on to the pavement remained intact. Once Ali heard that there were still shrapnel marks visible on the pillars outside the building, he told the chauffeur to make the GPO their first stop. Hopping out of the Mercedes, he ran his fingers along the stonework and took it all in.

'All that killing that went on was baaad!' said Ali to Monaghan. 'All wars are wrong. And all this time, it's still going on. This beautiful little country has paid its price for freedom and it shouldn't be divided. It's wrong, all killing is wrong.'

Croke Park was their next step. Ali wanted to get a proper look at the venue in the privacy and quiet afforded by early morning. Driving around the terraced streets, they came upon an elderly road sweeper, limping along, pushing a trolley containing his brush and shovel. It was the type of tableau that always appealed to Ali. He got out of the car and walked back to introduce himself. Monaghan heard the old man's jaw drop as Ali extended his hand and shook. The two moved over to the kerbside and sat down to continue their conversation. Ali and this street cleaner, shooting the breeze as dawn broke over Dublin. Deciding that his presence might spoil the moment, Monaghan stayed sitting in the back of the car and watched in amazement.

'Muhammad carefully raised the old man to his feet and bade him farewell,' wrote Monaghan. 'The old chap handed over a lucky charm to Muhammad, then asked for an autograph but not one of us had a pen. The old fella kept repeating: "God bless ya, Muhammad, God bless ya." As the chauffeur's foot hit the pedal, I looked back through the rear window. The old road sweeper was waving his cap in the air. Ali leaned out of the window and waved back. I slapped him on the knee and said: "Nice one, me old sunshine."'

4
Jackson Prison Blue

The same morning Ali arrived in Dublin to such a tumultuous welcome, his opponent's best attempts at diligence were being stymied. Rising at six, Al 'Blue' Lewis left his city centre hotel, the Ormonde, and jogged up the quays to Phoenix Park. With its rolling fields and network of roads, the park was the perfect location for a boxer to clock up some mileage. Only trouble was Lewis couldn't stop shivering. Nobody had told him he might find Ireland a little colder in summer than he was accustomed to and, accordingly, he hadn't worn enough clothes to work up a serious sweat. It was going to be that kind of day.

In the early afternoon, he and his camp had to drive around the city for close to an hour before negotiating their way to the handball alley at the back of Croke Park. Expecting to find a makeshift gym in which he could conduct his first proper sparring session, they found instead an empty handball alley. With nobody even able to rustle up a skipping rope, Lewis made do with some speedy shadow-boxing and Don Elbaum fumed to the handful of journalists present about the amateur nature of the set-up. The promoters' failure to provide a local to guide them to the premises had been bad enough but the lack of a training ring was something he'd never encountered in decades around the sport.

Lewis took all of this in his stride, telling reporters: 'As long as they make sure there is a ring for next week that's all I'm worried about.' Too laid-back to get riled up cheaply, he liked to laugh at the small stuff, and it wasn't as if he didn't know what to expect. He'd glimpsed Ali's world from the inside and knew exactly the way the build-up was likely to play out. Ali was the cash cow and the promoters would cater for his every whim and fancy while allowing Lewis to make do with second-best. Being second-best to Ali didn't bother him one whit. He didn't have to be told that it was Ali's name on the poster that was underwriting their purses and here was one boxer who didn't begrudge his opponent one red cent of his six-figure fee.

Their paths had first crossed in June 1967. Five days before a judge in Houston found him guilty of unlawfully refusing induction into the US Army, Ali boxed a couple of three-round exhibitions at Cobo Hall in Detroit. Lewis was his first opponent, a former Golden Gloves champion in the city but still a neophyte in the professional ranks. For him, the thrill of getting into the ring with Ali in his home town was amplified by the knowledge he was being paid $100 per round for the privilege.

'It was good money, especially since I was a nobody and he let me go three rounds with him,' says Lewis. 'I fought hard and he could have got mad at me and got me outta there, but he didn't. I know now he could have done that, but he didn't, he let me look good that day. He did me a helluva favour and I told him that if he ever got his licence back, I'd go anywhere to help him out.'

The opportunity for payback came in Miami Beach in October 1970 when Lewis was part of the sparring rotation assisting Ali's preparations for the comeback against Jerry Quarry. The day before the party was due to leave for Atlanta, Ali wanted to steel himself for any Quarry offensive on his body so he invited Lewis to pound his stomach repeatedly. Holding his hands above his head, he kept egging him on: 'Hit me, Hit me.' Carrying out those instructions to the letter, Lewis gave him his best shot straight to the ribs.

Ali hit the ropes before sliding to the canvas. At first, many observers thought he was hamming it up, exaggerating the effect to add a little melodrama to a routine spar. But in his autobiography, Ali talks about the pain of that blow 'shooting through bones, up the spine, up the back of my head'. Ever the performer, he managed to wink at the spectators in an effort to

43

make light of the injury and they continued sparring a while longer. When the workout finally ended, a concerned Angelo Dundee escorted him hurriedly to the dressing room. As they examined the damage done, 'Blue' Lewis came in to apologise.

'I didn't know you weren't ready, you told me to throw them in hard,' said Lewis.

'If you didn't, I'd get another sparring partner,' responded Ali.

For all Ali's bravado, there was consternation in the camp that night. A broken rib would have meant postponing the Quarry fight and nobody knew how difficult it might be to arrange another bout. To prevent the press getting wind of any negative reports, Ali's physician, Dr Ferdie Pacheco, arranged a midnight consultation at the offices of Dr Carlos Llanes, a radiologist who counted the Miami Dolphins among his clients. The X-rays showed heavy bruising but no fracture. Nobody was more relieved than Lewis whose bit part in the pre-fight drama wasn't over yet.

Early the following morning, he was among a group killing time in Ali's hotel room as he packed to get ready for his flight to Atlanta. Lewis just happened to be nearest the door when the knock came and eager to be of help, he jumped to answer it. A man handed him two white boxes, festooned with red and green ribbons and left in a hurry. Lewis marched back into the room, the bearer of good tidings. 'Someone here with some packages for the Champ!' he said. The gifts were addressed to 'Mister Cassius Clay from Georgia'. Lewis started to take the wrapping off one of them and joked: 'Who knew I wanted cake for breakfast?' Then the blood started to seep out on to his hands and he hurled the boxes to the ground.

A black chihuahua had been decapitated and boxed in order to better hammer home the fact that many Georgians were not exactly pleased that Ali's first comeback fight would take place in their state. The bleeding torso and severed head were accompanied by a note containing the Confederate flag and the message: 'We know how to handle black draft-dodging dogs in Georgia. Stay out of Atlanta!'

'It was a dog's head, man, a dog's head clean off the body,' says Lewis. 'They sent it to him all wrapped up like a present, and they delivered it right up into his room. The people who sent it were from Georgia, but that's Georgia, man. Georgia's down South, if you know what I mean. I'm from Detroit and Southerners are different than us.'

Beyond these cameos in the ongoing soap opera surrounding Ali, Lewis had a history of his own. One more international pit stop for 'The Greatest Show on Earth', for him this fight in Dublin was the culmination of an extraordinary journey. Because he lacked the name recognition or reputation of a contender, too many reporters appeared keen to portray him as a stumblebum waiting to be dismissed. They were missing the point entirely. That Lewis was actually in Ireland to take on the former heavyweight champion of the world represented a remarkable achievement in itself. How far he had travelled is only truly apparent when you look at where his voyage through life began.

'I came from Detroit's east side, a place they called "Black Bottom". You know the Brewster Projects and Hastings Street? It was dog eat dog down there, hell, yeah, it was rough. I had eleven brothers and three sisters, I was the baby boy and I had a sister younger than me. It toughened me up being the youngest boy. A couple of my older brothers fought but not to the level I did, they got into drugs and a lot of bad stuff and ended up in prison. My father wasn't a boxer although he had the name Joe Lewis all right, just the wrong spelling. He never fought except to try to whip our butts. He was a construction worker, a big strong man driving a truck and using machines.'

'Black Bottom' got its name in the early 1930s when a huge influx of African-Americans from down South moved into the area to see if the rumours about lucrative wages in the city's car factories were true. Back then, Detroit was as segregated as many Southern cities, and Verner Lewis gave birth to her twelfth son on 11 December 1942, six months before the city's simmering racial tensions exploded into thirty-six hours of rioting that left twenty-five blacks and nine whites dead. Back then, they used to say that the three best escape routes from the poverty of the Brewster Projects were boxing, basketball and music. The place was overrun with talent. Some was eventually discovered, a lot more went to rack and ruin in the unforgiving environment.

Joe Louis had trained in the Brewster Recreation Centre, lending the venue instant credibility and sparking a fistic dynasty that over the years spawned legendary trainers Eddie Futch and Emanuel Steward. Before the National Basketball Association amended its rule limiting black players, the Harlem Globetrotters used to regularly scout pick-up games in the gym for recruits. Berry Gordy, the founder of Motown Records liked to use the facility to work out and keep fit, and Smokey Robinson, Diana Ross and the Supremes all called the Brewster Projects home.

Young Al began sparring in the enormous footsteps of Louis from the age of seven. By the time he was in his early teens and reaching a point when he might have got more serious about the sport, the discipline afforded by the ring had lost its allure. He preferred the action on the street and started getting into trouble so quickly that he was forced to change his name. There weren't too many other Alvins around Brewster in those days and when somebody said: 'Alvin did it!' they always knew who to look for. Needing a nom de plume fast, he settled on 'Blue'. That it was his favourite colour was reason enough. Later, a story would gain credence that he was so-called because the baddest kid in every gang was nicknamed 'Blue'. He's always denied that, while openly admitting his badness was never in question.

'My mother got us moved out of Brewster and we moved to this new neighbourhood. There was a lot of white folks around that neighbourhood and a lot of prejudice. There were a lot of bars and nightclubs, and me and my friends would catch people in the side streets off Grand River when they were coming out of the clubs on their way home. I robbed a lot of folks back then. I robbed a lot of folks. There were a lot of gangs around that time. They weren't as dangerous as they are now. Now, the gangs shoot everybody, everybody got guns and they shoot at each other, they're all killers. None of this bang-bang for me. I didn't like weapons. I just used my fists.'

Those fists were to prove deadly enough weapons and after a fashion, the law caught up with him.

'I robbed a white guy and he died in hospital later. They said I did it anyway. It was a year later when they arrested me and asked me whether I did it. Now at that time I didn't know what I did last week, never mind a year earlier. He died from head injuries in hospital and the judge said I was the cause of him going to hospital and he found me guilty. I couldn't really tell whether I was there or not, it sounded like me all right. I mean I robbed a lot of folks back then so it could have been. Anyway, I got sentenced to twenty to thirty-five years in jail. I was seventeen.'

He was already familiar with Jackson State Prison. His brothers, Patrick and Ed, had spent time there and he'd been to visit. Seeing it from the other side was different and that first night alone in his cell scared him so much he decided to try a new tack. The juvenile delinquent, sent down for his part in a robbery where the victim died because he wouldn't hand over the ninety-seven bucks in his possession, set out to become the model prisoner. He avoided fights, not an easy task inside, sang in the prison choir and started sparring in the gym. A decade after he'd first put on gloves, the sparring went so well that he put his name forward for the prison championship and ended up winning it five years in a row.

'I didn't get real big until I went to prison. When doing robberies I only weighed 153 lb and was about five ten. All of a sudden I was six foot four and 220 lb. I didn't lift no weights or nothing, I was just naturally strong. I had to fight four or five times a year to take the title. Those fights were something, all the inmates sitting around the ring watching us. There were Mafia there, KKK, Arabs, white guys, black guys, Hispanics, everybody sitting with their own kind. In Jackson, you had to watch yourself outside the ring, in the ring you were safe enough. I fought this big white guy one time, a Mafia dude, Marty Lardy. The Mafia reckoned he could fight so I called the round I'd put him down in. They didn't like that I told them he'd go down in two. I knew he hadn't ever fought nobody before, he was just a strong weightlifter who weighed about 270. Once I found out he was a weightlifter, I knew he'd be too slow for me. I killed him inside two, and the Mafia guys went crazy. He was a bad mother but he was tall and tight and couldn't box.'

One day, somebody handed Lewis a boxing magazine and he lay on his bed reading the story of Sonny Liston's life. It set him thinking. If only he wasn't in for such a long stretch. If only he'd not led the life he had. Unbeknown to him, word of his exploits in the prison ring had filtered all the way back down to Detroit. In a city consumed by the sport, even the minutiae of intra-convict bouts are the stuff of debate. Steve Eisner, the owner of a chain of drive-in movie theatres, had been managing a few fighters around town when a business associate assured him that the best unknown heavyweight in the country was an inmate of Jackson Prison. He was intrigued enough to want to go see for himself.

'This guy Merle, he owned a factory but he was a real boxing buff, so he gets us passes and we go up to the penitentiary,' says Eisner. 'The day we're there, Lewis is fighting Billy Pickett, a good pro who had a truncated career due to his nefarious outside activities. Billy Pickett's in the ring and he knows what he's doing and then there's 'Blue' Lewis who is just raw talent, a real rough diamond with little or no formal training. I'm sitting behind Merle and he turns to me and says: "I'll bet you a hundred bucks Lewis wins." I said: "I don't have a hundred, let's make it twenty-five." So Lewis comes roaring out of his corner, Pickett jabs, makes a few moves and suckers him into being right in line for a left hook, then a straight right and down goes Lewis. He looks flat out, dead. I turn to Merle and say: "This, you brought me all the way up here for this?" Merle doesn't flinch. He says: "I'll bet you twenty-five more he gets up and twenty-five beyond that that he knocks Pickett out." "Bullshit!" I said. "You're on." I turn around to see Lewis running across the ring, practically throwing the referee out of his way and attacking Pickett with all kinds of weird-angled punches from every place they could come. A surprised Pickett gets knocked out through the ropes of the ring. Afterwards, Merle gets a prison guard to take me and him down into the dressing room and we talk to Lewis. Even though I know he's in for at least twenty years, I hand him my card and tell him to look me up if he ever gets out. Really, I'm thinking to myself: "What a pity, this guy is only twenty or something and he's got some talent and his life is already over.'"

In the summer of 1965, a group of inmates rioted to protest at conditions inside Jackson. The prison was so big that Lewis didn't even know what the problem was until he found himself being corralled back to his cell by warders anxiously seeking to isolate the trouble. When the noise died down, seven black prisoners were holding a white doctor and an inspector hostage. The leader of the group was a lifer who knew Lewis and thought he could be trusted as a mediator.

'I think the prisoners sent for me cause they knew I was tight with the prison commissioner because of the boxing,' says Lewis. 'That's why they wanted to see me. It kind of blew my mind, man, to be asked to do that, but I went and listened to their grievances. They wanted to see a newspaper reporter from Jackson, a reporter from Detroit, and they wanted to see a prisons' inspector or else heads were going to roll. While they were telling me this, there was a guard with me standing off to the side listening but hiding. I went back to the commissioner and they got to air their grievances, handed over the hostages and that was the end of it. Those prisoners were all in the middle of long sentences so I suppose you could say I played my part in saving those guys' lives.'

Shortly before Christmas that year, he was summoned to the commissioner's office. The first words he heard were: 'Remember you did that favour for me back in the summer.' Seven years before he was eligible for his first parole hearing, Al 'Blue' Lewis had received an early release. His crucial role in the hostage crisis had brought him to the attention of the authorities and when they started asking questions around the prison, every employee spoke glowingly of his general behaviour and attitude.

'He was highly recommended by everyone in the institution,' Gus Harrison, then director of Michigan's Department of Corrections told the *Detroit News*. 'He had a programme. He had some friends. He wasn't one of these in-and-outers. He didn't have a long string of arrests and convictions. I was impressed with him, his behaviour and his appearance. I don't know what would have happened if he hadn't been there [during the riot] but I know that he was there and nothing happened to me.'

His spotless record and willingness to put himself on the line to help others in a time of genuine crisis had convinced them he deserved a second chance.

'The commish told me to call my momma,' says Lewis. 'I didn't even know the number to call and they had to look it up for me. I was crying calling my mother to tell her I was coming home. I'd done five years, six months and two weeks. I remembered every minute and I knew I was blessed to be coming out the way I was. I told the commish right there: "I'm going to work and I'm going to box and I won't be back."'

He caught a bus to Detroit on 7 January 1966 and barely recognised the place he'd left behind. So many of the landmarks of his childhood had already been demolished. Hastings Street, one of his old hang-outs, had been turned into an eight-lane freeway. Trying to make good on his promise to go straight, he wanted to start boxing again as quickly as possible. The Liston story had been playing over and over in his head since he heard he was getting out, and one of the first things he did was head over to Brewster to see about getting some sparring in at the gym.

'I'm about to walk out of the gym after a training session with some of my fighters there,' says Eisner. 'I walk straight into this huge black guy and he looks down at me and says: "You don't remember me, do you?" I say: "No, frankly I don't remember you." He picks me up by the arms so I'm looking him right in the eye and says: "It's me, 'Blue'." "Oh, for God's sake," I said. "Put me down, I know the head of the prison system, I can get you back in." I figured he must have escaped and I offered to take him back up to Jackson myself. "I'm not going back," he says, and he picks me up again to tell me the story of the riot.'

Eisner became his manager, and Luther Burgess, a Brewster veteran, took over his training. As a featherweight, Burgess had gone ten rounds with Willie Pep in 1948 and was now proving himself an even better trainer than he'd been a fighter. Lewis needed more than just technical coaching. He wanted a trainer who kept him busy enough to stay out of trouble and Burgess proved a perfect fit. 'He was my guardian angel,' says Lewis. 'My father, my big brother, I can't describe what he did for me.' Within three months of leaving prison, Lewis reached the final of the Detroit Golden Gloves.

In Cobo Hall in downtown Detroit that night, there were some strange sights and sounds to behold. Growing up in Brewster, every kid had a distinctive whistle by which they were able to summon their pals to their side quickly if things turned bad. Nobody had a catcall quite like Lewis though, and when he entered the arena, his supporters did their best to mimic that unique shrill he used to produce. Yards from the ring, he himself noticed more familiar faces. Two rows had been taken by prison guards from Jackson. Everyone who could get the night off had made the trip down to the city to watch him fight. The kid they'd first met as one more gang-banger from the street had turned into a prospect worth following in their spare time.

'That was a helluva honour for me to see them there that night,' says Lewis. 'Even before I stopped the riot, I had made a few friends among the guards. I take people as I find them and I figure it was that since I treated them like they were gentlemen, they treated me like I was a gentleman. They always treated me like I was somebody.'

With support like that, there was no way he could lose, and his victory in the Detroit Golden Gloves yielded him a ticket to the National Finals in Kansas City.

'In the nationals, we told "Blue" to watch out for this guy's right hand,' says Eisner. 'We told him to keep his left hand jabbing, keep his right hand high, and block that left hook. But we hadn't time to really teach him too much and he ended up getting knocked down in the second. Now, "Blue" was knocked down maybe fifteen times in his career but he got up each time. On this occasion, he gets up perfectly all right but the ref stops the fight and awards it to the other guy on a KO. "Blue" was furious and as the microphone came down for the national radio audience, he shouted, "You motherfucker!" That was the end of his amateur career. We wanted him to have another two years as an amateur but that was the end of that. Luther Burgess said to me: "We got to turn the man pro."'

Lacking the ready cash necessary to finance a contender's development, Eisner had got Ted Ewald, a wealthy car dealer from Grosse Pointe, involved in the management side, and Lewis's professional debut came against Art Miller in Canton, Ohio, on 21 June 1966. Not even a year since Jackson had been convulsed by the riot, he was getting paid to box. He knocked Miller out in the first and soon established a pattern for ending fights in a hurry. Between June and December 1966, he notched up six KOs on the way to eight consecutive victories and never stopped hustling, his attitude best exemplified by his first-round victory over Vic Brown in his fourth pro fight.

'I was supposed to fight Buster Brownfield one night in a four-rounder for fifty bucks,' says Lewis. 'In the main event, Buster Mathis was getting $1000 to fight Vic Brown over ten rounds. Brown was a southpaw and Mathis didn't want no part of him so they asked me would I switch opponents for another $75. Hell, for $125 I'd fight him if he had three left hands. I was desperate man.'

Even as the standard of his opposition improved, he continued to impress, easily winning his next six. The wheels came off slightly in December 1967 when Bob Stallings dropped him in the seventh, but just five months later he won the rematch.

'At that stage, "Blue" was a fiercesome sight in the ring,' says Eisner. 'Don Elbaum was a friend of mine who did matchmaking and promoting in Ohio and he came in to help us. We got to the point where "Blue" was a pretty good fighter and we wanted to prove how good he was. Eduardo Corletti from Italy was number two or three in the world and Elbaum suckered him into going in with "Blue". "Blue" knocked him out right through the ropes in the second round. That was July 1968 and that got him nationally ranked and brought him to the attention of people.

'He then had two fights with Leotis Martin. He lost the first because he hadn't trained hard enough. He was ahead on points and then he ran out of gas. The second time, he won the fight. But the referee was jealous of Ted Ewald's money and didn't like the fact "Blue" was a convict so he awarded it to Martin. Those defeats were a big slight on his record and it was sad that some people couldn't look past the fact he was an ex-con. He was in with good fighters all the time, he destroyed Cleveland "Big Cat" Williams up at the Fairgrounds in Detroit. We got "Blue" to the point where he'd become a real talent except he had no left jab. He did this thing that they always do in the Joint, he hung the left hand down and waved it at you but he wouldn't hook with it. He just wanted to throw the right because he was more comfortable with that.'

After the second loss to Martin, Lewis's career began to falter. He'd become the victim of his own reputation and fought just six times in twenty-seven months. Not a big enough name to get the serious money at the top of the bill but considered way too dangerous for savvy promoters to risk their good prospects on. Any smart manager didn't want their man in against somebody who with one punch could lose them more lucrative pay days down the line. With no marquee value, he struggled to make a living and yet had gained real respect from his fellow fighters.

When Ali bumped into Sonny Liston one day at the state

building in Sacramento where they were both hoping to get licences to fight in California, they got to talking about their previous encounters. In the course of their conversation, Ali mentioned how Jimmy Ellis had nearly broken his ribs in sparring just before the rematch in Maine. He thought he was revealing some big secret to his old rival. 'They came and told me about it,' said Liston. 'But I didn't believe it. I'd never known Ellis to hit hard. If they'd said somebody like "Blue" Lewis or Cody Jones had done that, I'd have believed it.'

The fact Liston and Ali both rated Lewis as a 'banger' is the reason why one boxer even paid for the privilege of not fighting him.

'Lewis is the guy Buster Mathis once paid $6,000 rather than fight,' wrote Dick Young in the *New York Daily News*. 'Buster had run out on the bout with "Blue" and was suspended. To regain his licence, he was told he must meet the obligation. After all, it had cost Lewis money to train. Mathis had a good money shot with Ali if he could get the licence back but if he fought Lewis, he'd get belted out and there would go the Big One. So the people handling Buster bought off Lewis for the six Gs.'

In October 1971, Lewis flew to Buenos Aires to take on Oscar Bonavena. Just ten months earlier, Bonavena had lasted fourteen rounds with Ali in Madison Square Garden before succumbing in the fifteenth. This was to be his comeback fight. That Lewis was prepared to take on the Argentinian on his home turf was evidence of his willingness to go anywhere to fight. It also demonstrated how desperate he'd become. Decent, paying bouts were proving so hard to come by that he had to take on one of the more difficult assignments in the sport. Beating an Argentinian in Argentina is almost impossible. He had Bonavena down three times in four rounds and was cruising until getting disqualified in the seventh of alleged use of the head.

'I killed Bonavena, man, I killed him,' Says Lewis. 'Don't get me wrong, he did knock me down but I was slapping him around. I was so much bigger than him and he just knocked me down 'cause I got casual. I said: "You ain't hitting me no more like that." I beat him so much in that ring that he called the referee and told him that I cut him in the eye with my head. I didn't need to use my head I was beating him so well as it was. It was a home-town decision and Jeez, that's a dangerous country. There were wars and rioting the whole time we were there, all day long it was fine, then at night, there was screaming and shouting. The only time I was ever scared was when I was in Argentina, I was scared of that country, boy, it was a crazy place. Every day we had to keep moving gyms because of the rioting. I didn't like Argentina one bit.'

After the controversial loss to Bonavena, Lewis was idle for nearly ten months. He sold another piece of his contract to Chuck Nary, a shady character out of Charleston, South Carolina. With Eisner, Ewald, and now Nary all retaining a hold of some sort on Lewis, progress was always going to be difficult. The last thing a fighter who had become a fully-fledged member of boxing's 'who needs them?' club (those hard-hitters who are capable of defeating anyone on a given night and therefore best avoided) needed was a complicated promotional situation. It appeared that at twenty-nine his chances of even snagging a half-decent pay day were fast disappearing. That was when Elbaum rang him up and asked him if he wanted to go to Dublin to fight Muhammad Ali.

Accompanied by his brother Pat and Ray Anderson, a light-heavy out of Philadelphia who had been hired as his sparring partner, he flew to Ireland. He didn't know much about the country. He'd heard about the troubles in Belfast but figured no place could be as scary as Buenos Aires in the grip of sustained civil unrest. First night in the Ormonde hotel, he kept looking out the window and wondering when darkness would fall. The fact that it stays bright in Ireland in the summer until past ten in the evening was only one of the surprises.

'I was out in the country and saw these cows, they were some big old cows, cows the size of horses, man, I saw them and I says to myself: "Those are big old cows!" I walked across to check whether it was even a cow but it was, eating the grass and all. This big tall cow with big titties on it and everything. It was very different from old Detroit. I mean, Dublin was all white too. I hadn't seen nothing black in the whole town except me and my people. Then I saw this real nice little black kid in among all the white folks. That just blew my mind, this little girl so lightly skinned that she could have been white but when I looked at her real good, she was definitely black. I was just glad to see that. I was surprised that I met no racists there. I was very surprised. Everybody looked at me strange but they treated me very well. Very well. Whatever I asked for, it was given to me. I was real important that week. Some of them were treating me like I was the champ.'

Not everybody was that way inclined. At their first joint press conference, Ali went into his usual spiel about his popularity at the box office.

'The people will be there,' proclaimed Ali. 'I don't know why but there's just something about the name Muhammad Ali, the place just fills up. They can write what they want, they can say what they want but they will come from all over the world—'

'To see us,' interjected Lewis.

'To see us?' replied Ali with a hint of exaggerated disdain.

'Remember now!' warned Lewis in vain.

'They're coming to see me and part of you,' said Ali, the delivery perfectly timed to send the audience into raptures and remind his opponent of his place.

5

The Greatest Hurler Who Never Lived

I

Wednesday's morning newspapers had advertised 1.30 p.m. as the starting time for Muhammad Ali's first training session at Croke Park. Long before then, people began milling outside the handball alley at the back of the stadium, eager to gain a good vantage point from which to catch their first glimpse of him in action. Filing into the hall to take their seats, they could reflect that 50p was a fair enough admission charge for what they were about to receive. It wouldn't be long now before the glass wall that served as the back end of the court would be the only thing separating Him from them. They'd be close enough to see him perspire, watch those feet dance and marvel at the awesome speed of his hands.

Again and again and again, they looked at their watches. Soon, it was nearer two than one thirty. The natives were growing kind of restless and, unknown to them, Ali still hadn't left Opperman's on the far side of town. At ten past two, their patience received a stay of execution. The workers who had been busy hammering away at the ring silenced their tools and a steady stream of boxing equipment began to materialise. When a man entered carrying the bell, there were gasps of expectation. He was followed by a group manhandling a heavy bag into place and suddenly the handball alley took on the appearance of a real gym. Fifteen minutes before three, there was an announcement that Ali's arrival had been delayed by traffic congestion but was now really, genuinely, honest-to-God, imminent.

The clock had just ticked past three when the black Mercedes ferrying Ali began struggling to find a safe passage through the crowd outside. Within a minute, the car's Mercedes Benz logo was swiped as a souvenir by a couple of young boys who merged back into the crowd before the driver could even toot his horn. Eventually, Mara Lynn took the matter in hand. The epitome of Fifth Avenue glamour in her crocodile boots, she climbed on to a chair to plead with the people 'to let him through'. Not quite Moses parting the Red Sea, but effective nevertheless. It was a slightly subdued Ali who finally entered the handball alley.

'The big man had been preceded by an oddly dressed collection of people that included Rock Brynner, a son of the man with no hair,' wrote Con Kenealy in the following day's *Irish Independent*. 'Muhammad was strangely quiet to those of us who had only seen and heard him on television. There was no remark at all, he just went in wearing a sweatshirt.'

Luis Sarria, his Cuban masseur, carefully laid the bandages on top of the ropes. Angelo Dundee took them and wrapped his hands with the same precision that had informed his work during their twelve years together. Then Ali moved to the speed bag and began massaging it for the benefit of the photographers massed nearby. He was sporting the top half of a rubber suit to assist his sweating, and from a couple of yards away, his brother Rahamam, decked out in a double-breasted suit and tie, with spats on his feet, watched his every action with the same intensity as the short-sleeved spectators on the other side of the glass. After a few minutes, he moved away from the speed bag, loosened the elastic of his waistband and allowed a sluice of sweat to pour down from under his top and splash on to the ring floor.

'It was during those few moments that incredibly I found Muhammad Ali looking directly down at me,' wrote Marie Corr in the *Irish Press*. 'Plucking up the courage and momentarily forgetting my total ignorance of boxing, I found myself asking him questions. Metaphorically, I was kayoed. Somehow it hadn't occurred to me that an acknowledged champion who loudly and repeatedly proclaims his own beauty and greatness could be anything other than a shallow braggart. What a pleasant surprise to discover that Muhammad Ali, alias Cassius Clay, is unquestionably a superior human being. That he is a handsome specimen of a human being goes without saying. What astonished me, however, is his colouring, which, to me, looked no darker than that of a Spaniard or a southern Italian. I was to discover that this superb boxer and extrovert showman has a thoughtful, serious side to him. Allied to this is his courteous manner and dignified bearing, which all combine to give an impression of a very fine worthwhile character.'

Having entertained Corr for a few minutes with standard-issue answers to enquiries about diet, Islam and Vietnam, it was now time to put the gloves on for his first serious spar since fighting Quarry on 27 June. In the other corner stood Basil 'Bunny' Sterling, a good enough middleweight to win British, European and Commonwealth titles, his quickness had won him the job of warming Ali up. Twenty-four years old and admirably enthusiastic, he wore sparkling new white boots, the gleaming shine from which contrasted with Ali's old, mud-splattered shorts. From the bell, Sterling went on the offensive, delivering a flurry of jabs to Ali's head and at ringside. One of the watching reporters summed up the sparring partner's overexuberance perfectly: 'Ah, Bunny's bid for fame!'

Ali accepted the initial assault without flinching, perhaps feeling he needed to remind his body of what this whole business was about. The rest of the first round passed without incident. In the second, however, Sterling unwittingly incurred the wrath of Ali. The watching journalists noticed a change in his demeanour as he began beating up on the middleweight. At one point, Sterling was clung against the ropes receiving blow after blow to the left side of his head. He'd made one fatal error and for the remainder of the round he had to pay the price. When Ali got back to his corner, he loosened the elastic band again to drain off the sweat and Dundee warned him to cool down.

'Bunny happened to catch Ali's eye with his thumb and Ali punished him for that,' says his trainer George Francis. 'And afterwards, I went to the dressing room and asked what happened and Angelo says: "He thumbed him in the eye." It wasn't intentional because you'd never do that to the big man but Ali opened up on him for a bit then, as if to say: "Don't you dare do that!" Just to put him in his place. But it was an accident, the truth is Bunny broke his thumb early in his career and could never actually close his thumb. And the rules are that you are supposed to be able to make a complete fist. So basically he boxed with his thumb sticking out. I couldn't say that then but that's what happened when he thumbed Ali. I couldn't go up and explain he had a dodgy thumb because I should have had it broken and bent round long before that.'

It was unfortunate that Sterling, of all people, should get on the wrong side of Ali because his own story was also one of triumphing over adversity and bucking the establishment. After his parents left Jamaica to work in London in the late forties, he'd been reared by relatives until following across the Atlantic at the age of eight. When he began boxing professionally in the mid sixties, black fighters were still a novelty in rings around Britain, and though never destined for greatness, he left a unique imprint on the sport. Despite suffering questionable decisions in his first three pro fights, he kept improving until the only thing standing between him and a shot at a British title was his immigrant status. Francis petitioned the British Boxing Board of Control to change its rules and when it did, Sterling became the first immigrant to hold the British middleweight crown. A game fighter, he took Ali's flash of temper in his stride.

'He's about fifteen stone and a guy like me just cannot push him away,' said Sterling conveniently ignoring the beating he'd received. 'I felt great all through the workout and Ali looks really strong to me. It is against me that I'm using new boots today.'

John Conteh, another Francis fighter and a flatmate of Sterling's in Muswell Hill, climbed through the ropes next. Ranked number-three heavyweight in Britain that summer, the twenty-one-year-old boasted an Irish ancestor just like Ali, his maternal great-grandfather having departed Cork for Liverpool around about the same time Abe Grady was leaving Clare for America. Taking Dundee's advice, Ali was in more playful mood with his second sparring partner. For the benefit of the crowd, he put the gloves over his eyes and willingly took a few heavy shots off the up-and-coming Scouser.

'This is my first time to spar with Ali and it is great to be in there with him,' said an excited Conteh. 'You can learn more mixing with him in a session like this than from any other man in the game.'

After two rounds, Conteh was replaced by Joe Bugner.

'He is a Viking, 6′ 4″ with a head of little blond curls,' wrote Elgy Gillespie in the *Irish Times*. 'His angel blue eyes are framed in a helmet with little jutting crescent pieces. He wears pale blue suede boots and cherry red mitts. In contrast with Ali's absolutely hairless skin, he is covered with golden down. Ali gives Bugner lots of exercise and good theatre, snorting like a bull; again he preserves his strength by warding off his blows with his arms and pressing him against the ropes, almost leaning on him with the look of exhaustion. By the third round, Bugner is white-faced with effort, bent backwards on the ropes, again he wriggles out so he can bash Ali with a few dog-tired blows. Spectators at ringside get out of the way lest Ali breaks Bugner's nose and blood spout over the watchers. Both look relieved when the bell goes and yet I'm assured, Ali could finish him off with a few thoughtful blows.'

In 1970, Bugner's manager Andy Smith had paid £420 for the privilege of getting his fighter some sparring experience with Ali in Miami. The two years since then had seen Bugner win and lose the British, Commonwealth and European heavyweight titles and the trip to Dublin was another step in his rehabilitation. With a European title fight against Jürgen Blin already fixed for London in October, he was due to spend a week as Ali's sparring partner-in-chief before fighting Canada's Paul Nielsen on the Croke Park undercard.

'I have sparred on three occasions with Ali,' said Bugner. 'We were warming up today and tomorrow the work will be faster. It will get progressively faster as we get nearer the fight. This is the ideal way to get timing and strength going well together on the big day.'

When the sparring ended, the real fun began, Ali transforming himself from earnest pugilist to crowd-pleasing entertainer. As he returned to the speed bag, he began joshing with the crowd. Unfortunately, the sound proofing of the handball alley didn't help him any. Returning to his favoured theme of how Frazier was too ugly to be champ, he informed them that the champ should 'be a pretty thing like me', primping his hair as he spoke. This was a sight gag and they cheered their approval. Buoyed by that reaction, Ali shouted: 'You want Frazier to win?'

'Yeah!', they replied, obviously hoping that was the answer to the question he'd posed.

Ali was not amused by the acoustics playing havoc with his routine. He tried again, his voice pitched louder than before and the questions simplified.

'Are you for "Blue" Lewis?'

'Noooh!'

'Are you for Ali?'

'Yeeaaah!'

All through the amateur dramatics, Lewis sat long-faced in his dressing room as he had done since one thirty. Informed that he could only train when Ali had finished, he'd endured the same earlier wait as the fans outside, like a supporting actor waiting for the studio's marquee name to arrive on set. Sensing his dissatisfaction, he was cornered by some journalists eager to up the ante.

'I've heard all that crap before,' said Lewis, as he listened to Ali's strained conversation with the crowd. 'Listen to all that crap. The guy's not a fighter. He's an actor. He didn't get to Frazier and he won't get to me. He's just inflating his own courage. Me, I'm ready for the kill.'

The fun and games hadn't ended yet. On his way out, Ali spotted Ray Anderson lurking in the corridor. In Ireland principally to assist Lewis, and perhaps wangle a spot on the undercard for himself, Anderson was a ranked light-heavy who was a regular sparring partner of Joe Frazier's. This last entry on his CV gave Ali the excuse he needed.

'Get out of here before I bust your nose,' he shouted at Anderson. 'You have been sent over by Frazier to spy on me. You go back and tell ugly Joe Frazier that I'm fit and ready and waiting to get back my title.'

The spectators loved the ersatz anger in his voice although the press could see a grin break across Ali's face as he moved towards the exit. Five weeks later, he'd happily box an exhibition against Anderson in Baltimore, Maryland. The master of the hard sell knew that every hint of animosity, no matter how manufactured, was good for the promotion.

'Do not underestimate "Blue" Lewis,' said Anderson, playing his part in the marketing of the event. 'He has one hell of a punch and could worry Ali next Wednesday.'

The moment Ali left the ring, the majority of the crowd made for the doors too, the prospect of seeing him depart in a car more appealing than watching Lewis and Anderson get it on. Outside by the Mercedes, he rewarded their loyalty. Frustrating his handlers who knew he had a couple more important promotional engagements that day, he spent half an hour signing autographs and mugging for photos with the fans.

'After this performance,' quipped one local, 'all we can do is rename this place Muhammad Alley!'

II

In the picturesque Kilkenny village of Inistioge, Eddie Keher grew up in a house where his father Stephen, a keen fight fan, talked incessantly and evocatively about Jack Dempsey, Joe Louis and Gene Tunney. Catching the bug himself, Eddie had tracked the career of Muhammad Ali from the time he first began reading about an audacious braggadocio called Cassius Clay impacting on the heavyweight division. During the build-up to the first Sonny Liston fight in February 1964, Keher's abiding memory is one of trepidation.

Gleaning what information he could from newspaper coverage, he actually feared for the life of the young pretender against the 8-1 on favourite. Eavesdropping on a crackling radio signal all the way from Miami in what was early morning in Ireland, he tried desperately to visualise that contest, and was amazed that as the fight wore on Clay answered the bell for every new round. Eight years later, he found himself being invited to participate in a publicity stunt with the same fighter.

'I was working with Allied Irish Banks in Capel Street at the time and I got a phone call from Bob Ryan,' says Keher. 'He was the public relations manager with the bank and I think himself and the journalist Raymond Smith were doing some sort of thing to help sell the fight. They wanted to get some photographs into the papers and I suppose with it being held in Croke Park, they thought of me. They asked me would I come out and I was only too delighted with the opportunity to meet the man. I was going to the fight anyway, in fact, I'd already paid for my tickets.'

Any PR man worth his salt would have associated Keher with great days at Croke Park. Thirty years old, he was more than a decade into a hurling career of such achievement that he would eventually be selected at left corner forward on the sport's 'Team of the Century'. A deadly accurate scorer, the fourth of his six All Ireland medals would come that September when he orchestrated Kilkenny's famous comeback victory over Cork at the venue. On the phone, Ryan warned him to bring a couple of hurls and sliotars along to Ali's hotel for the photographs. A needless advisory. This was high summer and mid-season for Keher, a time when the dedicated amateur never travelled anywhere without the tools of his trade in the boot of the car.

'Muhammad was out training when I arrived. When he came in, he was in a sort of a rubbery suit, in a deep sweat and he had heavy boots on him. I was introduced and said hello. He was

64

very quiet at that stage, quiet but friendly. Not anything like the public image we knew of him. I don't know if they knew why I was there or who I was really. I suppose they were probably briefed about my Croke Park connection, if that meant anything to them. I didn't think he was as big as he was depicted to be, certainly not as tall as I imagined. He was a super-looking athlete and certainly as pretty as he looked on television in his prime. But I expected him to be towering because he was six three but he wasn't. He was a magnificent specimen of a man, very athletic-looking, in great looking shape. It was great to see him up close for the first time like that.'

The subdued demeanour disappeared when the group was ushered outside by photographers and journalists anxious to get the story of two sporting cultures colliding. Keher handed his spare hurl, three and some feet of planed ash to the bemused Ali.

'Well, he looked at it first and I was showing him how to hold it with two hands on the top of the hurl. I was catching it, going over to him putting his hands on it but he found that very difficult. They asked me to demonstrate a few basic hurling skills for him and now, as soon as he got into that mode, he became the public image again. He was utterly transformed, he started putting on this great show. As usual with something like that, he was treating it with a bit of fun, it was a bit of jollity for him, I suppose, after the training had been done for the day. I was trying to show him how to rise a ball and he made several efforts, and eventually got it up off the ground.

'I started showing him how to hit it but he was holding the hurl like a tennis racket. He couldn't get the two hands going on it at all. So I started hitting a few balls towards him, and he started trying to hit them back, that sort of stuff. They were asking me to show a few more skills, so I showed a few more things and eventually I started hitting them to him again. Then he started fencing me with the hurl, shouting at me: "Come on, come on." It was obvious he wanted to put on a show for the photographers. We had a great time, the crowd were lapping it up and the photographers and journalists were having a ball.'

Some of the reporters got a little bit carried away by the spectacle of Ali dabbling in the most uniquely Irish of sports.

'Muhammad Ali tried his hand at hurling yesterday and showed that given the time and coaching, he might well be "The Greatest" at our national game too,' wrote Raymond Smith in a slightly misleading intro in the following day's *Irish Independent*. 'The former heavyweight champion took one of the hurleys and was soon tapping the ball on the bas more adeptly than we could have imagined. Eddie demonstrated a solo run – and Ali quickly followed suit, and won applause all-round as he kept it going for four or five hops on the stick. He then tried his hand at rising the ball and later Eddie demonstrated for him one of the real arts of the game. I threw the ball head high to the Kilkenny star, he killed it in the air and brought it down to the hand all in one movement. Muhammad was obviously very impressed and kept asking for more. He confided to me that he had seen the game once on ABC's *Wide World of Sports* programme in the States and liked it.'

A committed hurling enthusiast, Smith was desperately anxious that Keher, still wearing his business suit, would showcase some of the game's more unique skills for the American contingent. He began directing Keher.

'Raymond Smith was telling me to do various things like hit a long ball up into the sky, and trap it on the hurl when it came down. Then they were throwing balls at me, and getting me to catch them on the hurl. I showed them the different styles of lifting the ball and, in fairness, Ali was interested in the various skills. And as soon as he saw how the hurl was used properly, he knew what had to be done all right. Ali tried a few different things and he did hit a ball, holding the hurl with one hand, a couple of times and got a big round of applause. It's not an easy skill to pick up and he wouldn't have the touch obviously enough. Any hurler will tell you that you'd have to get the feel for the thing.

'The thing I remember most about that part though is that Raymond Smith insisted on calling him Cassius Clay throughout, and I was afraid for my life at some stage, thinking he'd lash out at him over that. But no, he didn't react at all. I mean, I knew the stories of how angry he got with Ernie Terrell that time when Terrell insisted on calling him Clay. I was thinking to myself that Raymond Smith is a brave man to be calling this fellow Clay, well, either brave or foolish. Then I wasn't sure myself whether to call him Muhammad or Ali. I wondered which was the surname and which was the first name, I thought for some reason it was backwards and I wasn't sure what to call him.'

After jousting in this manner for more than half an hour, Ali eventually headed for his post-training shower but not before autographing the hurl and sliotar he had been dabbling with and gifting them to Keher. One of the photographers took a picture of him signing it and were he to sell the ball and the photo authenticating the signature today, Keher could probably make a tidy sum in the American memorabilia market. He never would. This is a man who on his first trip to New York in 1964 made a pilgrimage to Jack Dempsey's restaurant on Broadway specifically to seek out the former champ's autograph to bring home as a souvenir for his father in Kilkenny.

'I met Dempsey and that was a big thrill but I suppose half the world did really in that restaurant. To have met Ali in those circumstances was absolutely fabulous. Even after Ali left us, I was talking to Angelo Dundee for a good while. Dundee talked a lot about the first Frazier fight and he was making the point that Ali was out of boxing with the ban for three years. He was saying to me that if I was out of hurling for two or three years, it would be very hard to come back to my original form. It was just a general discussion about fitness and he was asking me as much about hurling as I asked him about boxing. It's just a wonderful memory to have.'

III

At one point in his conversation with Muhammad Ali, the Taoiseach, Mr Jack Lynch, turned to his visitor and told him: 'I hope to go to your fight on Wednesday next.'

'Since you're a busy man, I guess I'll get it over quickly,' said Ali.

'Oh, don't do that. It would spoil it,' replied the Taoiseach.

'Well, in that case, I'll let Lewis stay in the ring for more than one round.'

'I might get in there myself for a few rounds and keep the thing going,' countered the Taoiseach.

This wasn't just another Wednesday in the life of the nineteenth Dáil. The second-last sitting before breaking for summer recess the following evening, 12 July, was an especially busy day, the variety of items down for discussion in parliament reflecting the concerns of contemporary Irish society. Apart from parochial interests like a request for information about the proposed site of the Kerry County Hospital or the future fate of St Francis Xavier's Girls' School in Dublin, there was a demand for the removal of the tax on fluoride toothpaste, myriad questions about pig husbandry and repeated references to worrying unemployment statistics.

These were among the issues being debated when a convoy including Ali, his brother Rahaman, Paddy Monaghan, Angelo Dundee, Harold Conrad and Butty Sugrue swung through the gates of Leinster House that afternoon and caused pandemonium. Alighting from their cars, they were met by Paddy Burke, TD for Dublin County North, and the ubiquitous Chubb O'Connor, and their arrival prompted a degree of hysteria in the normally staid confines of government buildings. The newspaper accounts offer a flavour of the impact.

'Not since the late President John F. Kennedy was in Dublin in 1963 has a visitor from abroad been given as big a welcome at Leinster House as that accorded to Muhammad Ali when he went to the seat of parliament yesterday and met the Taoiseach,' said the *Cork Examiner*. 'The staff turned out in big numbers, the deputies turned out in big numbers and the press turned out to welcome the former heavyweight champion and he had to sign dozens of autographs before he was allowed to make his way down the corridors to the Taoiseach's office.

'The whole of Leinster House was in a tizzy,' reported the *Irish Press*. 'Elderly deputies, young senators, cooks, waitresses, clerks, parliamentary correspondents, Gardai, everybody, came running to see the boxer of the decade. Politics took a back seat.'

'Muhammad took Leinster House by storm', wrote Raymond Smith in the *Irish Independent*. 'Not since President Kennedy addressed both houses of the Oireachtas has the visit of one celebrity engendered such spontaneous excitement. Protocol was forgotten more than once during this whirlwind visit and it seemed to me that Muhammad must have shaken the hand of every member of the Cabinet as he made his way down the corridor to the Taoiseach's office, and later the hand of every leading member of the Opposition.'

It was the by now familiar figure of O'Connor who negotiated the passage of Ali and his entourage through the crowds to the inner sanctum where he was to meet the Taoiseach, a man who was having quite a good day himself. In the Dáil earlier, Lynch had challenged Fine Gael, the main opposition party, to move a writ regarding an August date for a crucial by-election in the Mid-Cork constituency. Chiding them for 'gamesmanship', he accepted the subsequent resolution in a bid to prove his government, its authority undermined by the lingering after-effects of the 1970 arms crisis, was not afraid to face the electorate.

Introducing Ali to Lynch, O'Connor mentioned that his boss had been an outstanding hurler and Gaelic footballer in his day.

'I played many times, Muhammad, on the field where you will be boxing next Wednesday night,' said the fifty-five-year-old Taoiseach, in a typically humble reference to his immense sporting pedigree.

From the fabled Glen Rovers' club on the northside of Cork city, Lynch had carved a unique place for himself in the annals of Irish sport. Wearing the blood and bandage colours of his native county, Lynch was on the Cork team which won an unprecedented four All Ireland hurling titles in a row between 1941 and 1944. A year later, he helped the Cork footballers triumph in the championship and when the hurlers emerged victorious again the following year, he became the only man ever to win six successive All Ireland medals. Selected at centre-field on hurling's 'Team of the Century', his idealistic view of sport was best encapsulated by a speech where he described the true hurler as 'a man of dignity, proud of his heritage, skilful, well disciplined and a sportsman'.

Using the public recognition he had gained on the field, and his training as a lawyer off it, Lynch entered politics in 1948 and succeeded Sean Lemass as leader of Fianna Fáil and Taoiseach eighteen years later. In a room normally reserved for meetings of the Irish Cabinet, his summit with Ali was witnessed by anybody with enough authority or neck to squeeze in the door and catch a glimpse of a small little piece of history. And historic it was.

In his own references to this event in *The Greatest*, Ali mentions that Lynch was surprised to discover that he was the first Western head of government to invite him to make an official visit. Up to that point, the only countries whose heads of state had been as welcoming towards Ali were Ghana, Nigeria, Egypt, Saudi Arabia, Libya, Mali, Kuwait, Somalia, Uganda, Pakistan, Indonesia, Sudan and Morocco. Most photographs show the two sporting giants from different eras and worlds sitting on a couch, the redoubtable Sugrue on a chair behind and between them, all three invariably laughing. Their conversation lasted half an hour and prolonged bouts of humorous banter were laced with occasional discussions of more serious matters, all of which were dutifully recorded by the journalists present.

'I have been to Britain, Germany and Switzerland but they did not honour me like this,' said Ali. 'This is the first time I have been invited to meet a top official like yourself. When I was a poor little boy back in Louisville, Kentucky, I looked upon the mayor as being a great man – now here I am today sitting beside the Prime Minister of this country. I am just an athlete, a fighter sitting here talking to a great man like you. I would love to be a leader of people some day – helping people.'

Proving adept as ever at saying the right thing to the right audience, Ali told Lynch he wanted to compliment the Irish people 'on their proud history of struggle for civil rights and justice'. As somebody whose own people had been 'underdogs for a long time', Ali explained that he knew exactly what such struggles entailed. However, he also admitted that even though he regularly read items in American newspapers pertaining to the conflict in Northern Ireland, he couldn't quite figure it out.

'What,' asked Ali, 'is this struggle all about?'

Lynch delivered a potted history of Ireland that only begged more questions from his guest.

'Why can't you talk about this situation with other world leaders?'

'We do, Muhammad,' answered Lynch. 'But it always seems to fall upon deaf ears because a little country like ours can't compete with the import-export economy of a nation with sixty million people. Britain has many other nations in the world depending on trade with her . . . There are other reasons too.'

'Well, I'll tell you something now,' said Ali. 'If President John F. Kennedy was alive today, there would not be one British soldier on Irish soil.'

According to Paddy Monaghan's memory of the event, there was full agreement in the room on that point, but Harold Conrad's recall of the political discourse is a tad more cynical. He reckoned that Ali spent fifteen minutes telling Lynch how to fix the problems in the North and the Taoiseach's polite response to this lecture was to suck on his pipe and listen intently.

The image of Lynch smoking his pipe and taking it all in certainly rings as true as some of the other jovial exchanges from the encounter. Mocking the more serious government business of the day, he told Ali that Fianna Fáil had something of a fight on their hands down in Mid-Cork and enquired as to the boxer's availability as a candidate.

'The most commonly heard crack around Leinster House yesterday was that the Taoiseach was meeting Ali to try to persuade him to stand as a Fianna Fáil candidate in the Mid-Cork by-election,' reported the *Cork Examiner*. 'It was learned later from a usually reliable source that Ali had shown interest at first but felt he must decline when told that he would have to retire from the ring if he were to be elected to the Dáil. "What a loss!" exclaimed one deputy.'

When it was time to leave, Ali patiently signed a slew of autographs for the politicians and journalists present, and as he prepared to go, Lynch couldn't resist one more paean to his visitor.

'I've met some great men in my time but you, you are the greatest.'

At this, Ali smiled, lowered his head in a gesture of exaggerated humility and replied: 'Oh, I knows it.'

With his ministers dissolving into hysterics, Lynch was laughing so hard he had to wipe away tears. Regaining his composure he continued to spar gamely.

'I shall be cheering for you at the fight, Muhammad.'

'What? Why, Al "Blue" Lewis told me that you said that to him also!'

Even on his way out the door, he couldn't resist keeping things going.

'Hey, they just found out that Al "Blue" Lewis is an Irishman!'

'I'll still be cheering for you,' said Lynch.

In a typically bizarre postscript to this portion of the visit, one politician couldn't resist name-checking his new-found friend in a contribution to a Dáil debate on the situation in Northern Ireland the following day. 'When Cassius Clay or Muhammad Ali – he actually gave me the pen as a souvenir – was here last night he said we were very decent people,' said Joseph Lenehan, a TD for Mayo North with a reputation for colourful contributions in the house. 'I would hold that view. We can agree with any type of religious people from anywhere.'

Following his audience with the Taoiseach, Ali took his party to the Dáil restaurant for a meal. Ordering himself two steaks, vegetables and Coca-Cola, he assured reporters this was his first food since morning and would be his last for twenty-four hours. He signed dozens of autographs for the restaurant staff and when one man rang home to tell his wife he was delayed at work, he put Ali on the line by way of explanation.

'Your husband is with the greatest boxer in the world,' said Ali to the presumably bemused spouse. 'Now you just don't go whuppin' him tonight 'cause he's with the champion.'

Sitting at the table, suitably entertained by an act he had witnessed so many times in so many different places before, Angelo Dundee sipped an Irish coffee enthusiastically and delivered his initial take on the country. 'This drink is good, you have something going for you in this. By the way, I hear you have a Bolton Street in Dublin. My wife [Helen Bolton] will be pleased to hear that. She's Irish on both sides of her family.'

Before leaving the restaurant, there was time for one more gag from his fighter.

'What were the last words the Lord uttered at the Last Supper?' asked Ali of his audience.

'Ali, it's very hard to say exactly what his last words were,' answered the ever-game Raymond Smith.

'Let every man pick up his own cheque!' said Ali.

From there, the party moved en masse to the Distinguished Visitors' Gallery to observe the proceedings of the Dáil for a few minutes. In the visitors' book, Ali signed his name and wrote underneath: 'The man who has no imagination stands on the earth. He has no wings. He cannot fly. Peace.'

On the way out of Leinster House, Ali was besieged again. This time, the crowd consisted of mainly young female clerks who had earlier failed to land an autograph or even a worthwhile close-up glimpse of the celebrity in their midst. While the *Cork Examiner* reported that most of the women were swooning in admiration of his physique and beauty, one unnamed female civil servant made a comment to the fighter which perhaps best caught the mood of the day.

'If you stick around here long enough, Ali,' she said, 'you might even become president.'

Whatever the chances of that, his first full day in the country had certainly left an impression on him. Back in Opperman's that night, he picked up the phone and tracked down Conrad to ask him a question.

'Where are all the niggers in this town?' he asked the man who brought him to Ireland.

'There aren't any,' replied Conrad.

6

Gun-runners and Rings of Steel

By the summer of 1972, Edenderry Boxing Club had found its latest home in a disused shoe factory flush by the banks of the Royal Canal. Hardly salubrious, the members liked to think that what they lacked in amenities, they compensated for with enthusiasm and ingenuity. Nearing the end of its fourth decade in existence, the club had become a staple of life in this midlands town thirty-seven miles from Dublin, a place where families had been sending their children for generations to learn how to box. Among the first arrivals all those years ago, the Brereton brothers were now generally regarded as the lifeblood of the place. When people outside of County Offaly thought of Edenderry boxing, Brereton was usually the first name that came to mind.

'It was my brother Sean who got the phone call from either Butty Sugrue or Terry Rogers, the president of the Irish Boxing Board of Control, asking him for a loan of our ring,' says Joe Brereton. 'It was a ring that we had built ourselves and it was a fine ring too. They wanted to use it as the training ring for the handball alley for the sparring sessions. We were only too delighted to do it. We went down to the club and loaded it up and brought it to Dublin on the back of an ould truck that Willie, another brother of mine who's died since, had at the time. He had the truck for the building work he'd be doing. Anyway, we got up there and we put it up from scratch. In fact, it gave us a bit of trouble. To get it into the ball alley we had to use ropes and a pulley to get it up over the wall. That was the only way to get in. Jesus, we had great crack doing it though.'

On the drive to Dublin, the Breretons had passed the time wondering how close they'd come to Muhammad Ali. As aficionados of the sport, they wanted to observe him training; as fans, they were just desperate to see him in person. They got more than they bargained for. After constructing the ring inside the handball alley, they hung back and watched him shuffle around the same canvas that a couple of nights before had been used by the children of Edenderry.

'We would have to be there to tighten the ropes when the training session ended,' says Brereton. 'He was great to watch train, you could see the footwork and I used to be amazed and mesmerised by it. He was a great man to talk too, of course. One particular morning we were up there and Muhammad came in, and he was flinging chairs and everything around the dressing room. He was shouting and roaring at the top of his voice, going on about how "Somebody had better get this ugly bum out of my dressing room! I don't want to see this bum anywhere near me!" He was talking about Al "Blue" Lewis and I don't think Lewis was even in Croke Park at the time. Let alone in the dressing room. Best of all, he turns around at the end to Angelo Dundee and a couple of others and says: "Boys, if that doesn't sell a few tickets, nothing will!" '

Sean Brereton was equally enamoured by the job. To be paid to work in close proximity to somebody who had held him in his thrall since the Rome Olympics was a privilege. At the end of one sparring session, Sean couldn't hold himself back any longer. He asked for, and received, permission to climb through the ropes. The fact that he won his first junior provincial title at nine didn't stop Ali laughing as he encouraged his latest opponent to "grow big, grow big" before the joke was over.

'The promoters' office was at the side of the Gresham and Ali came in there another day,' says Sean Brereton. 'Well, he was a thorough gentleman to everybody in there. He knew he was the best and when you met him he didn't go on the way he went on when he was on the television. Like, Joe Bugner thought he was the best thing since sliced pan and he sickened me with his whole attitude. The way Ali was going on, sure, you wouldn't think he was the superstar at all. I got so friendly with him over the course of the week that he invited me to go back to America with him. That's a solid fact. I was on the verge of going too only for Rock Brynner advising me not to go. He said: "Sean, look, when you're finished, what will you do over there, your marriage will be gone and everything." Honest to Jaysus, I was so big into the boxing and so wrapped up in the thing, I wanted to go.'

The contribution of Edenderry Boxing Club was destined for a place in Irish sporting folklore. Called up to provide a stop-gap training facility, the Breretons found their ring being used for the fight itself. This option became the best available after a few days wrangling, which highlighted the logistical difficulties starting to develop behind the scenes. The original contract stipulated the provision of a twenty-foot ring but, with only days to go, it emerged that there was no ring of that size to be found in the Republic. After some bright spark rang the King's Hall in Belfast and discovered their ring couldn't travel, a phone call was made to the Palace Barracks in Hollywood, County Down. At a time of heightened political sensitivity, bringing a ring down from a British Army facility in Northern Ireland added a new dimension to the problem.

'The only time in my years involved with Ali that there was any whisper of a threat against him was when we had to get the boxing ring down from the North,' says Rock Brynner. 'It was coming from a British military base and there was some threat made that the Orangemen were going to disrupt the fight and that there might be a bomb. The talk was they might try to impede the passage of the ring or there might be a bomb packed in the ring itself. There was some real concern for about half a day over that threat. We took some precautions about protecting the boxing ring as it travelled and stuff but I never really believed the threat. I never believed that anyone with any political cause would be stupid enough to injure Muhammad. I never felt safer in my life than when I was Muhammad's bodyguard.'

Earlier in the year, the Welsh and Scottish rugby teams had

refused to travel to Dublin for their Five Nations' matches against Ireland because of the increased political violence, and that summer, English showjumper Harvey Smith was the highest profile sportsman to receive letters warning him not to attend the Dublin Horse Show. Whatever the veracity of these particular threats against the ring, all those extra precautions were in vain. The new ring was measured out at less than sixteen feet inside the ropes and suddenly a bit of drama was turning into a crisis. Harold Conrad knew from experience that Angelo Dundee would never allow Ali to fight inside a space as small as that and a compromise was needed.

'Ali wouldn't even train in the ring from the North,' says Joe Brereton. 'He told them it was too small and that he wanted the training ring and nothing else. He was delighted with our ring, I knew that. Then we had to take it out of the ball alley and put it back in the park itself. We had a couple of other lads working with us as well and it must have taken us the guts of three hours just to get it out of the alley. It was worth it 'cause it was a great honour for the club to have our ring in there.'

Despite reports that one British bookmaker had slashed Lewis's odds of causing an upset from 25–1 to 5–1 on hearing news of the change in ring size, the manner in which the most essential piece of equipment for the fight had been secured turned into such a complicated and drawn-out process that it fuelled the belief that all was not going well. When reporters quizzed Conrad about ticket sales, he grew tetchy and ill-tempered. 'How the box office is going is the kind of stuff newspaper readers aren't interested in,' he told Neil Allen, correspondent of *The Times*. 'Only reporters ask questions like that.' Hindered perhaps by initial scepticism about whether Ali really was coming to Dublin, there was no great early rush on tickets and the chaos surrounding the training facilities and now the ring didn't inspire confidence.

'I wasn't financially involved but I was asked in to help out the promotion,' says Barney Eastwood. 'Conrad got in touch with me to see if I could help them because I was heavily involved in professional boxing in Belfast at that time. Naturally enough I said I would as long as I could get a couple of guys on the bill. As soon as I became involved, I realised the operation was being very badly organised. It was a classic case of there being far too many cooks. And it wasn't all Butty's fault either because the Americans had a lot to do with the organising of it.'

Anybody who'd been around boxing fights of this stature before realised this one was taking on a unique flavour.

'It was a very dinky operation,' says Brynner. 'There was a lot of worry that week. There was no way that Muhammad wouldn't get paid, that was a sure thing, no one was going to stiff him. But there was a constant shortage of money, it was literally envelopes being rushed around with cash in them. Not at all what we were used to. At most Ali fights we never saw money or ever heard talk of money. That all just happened in the background. In Dublin, it was people sitting in lobbies, waiting for envelopes. Sugrue seemed to be literally paying step by step for the fight with bar receipts. There were envelopes of cash coming in to pay for stuff and the cash still smelled of Guinness.'

Budd Schulberg had been around professional boxing for longer than Brynner and he could see that his old pal Conrad wasn't relishing this particular caper.

'Hal was having a very tough time,' says Schulberg. 'He was complaining and bitching to me all the time that these people didn't know what the hell they were doing and they were never going to get this fight put on. He was like that all through the week right up to the fight. He was worried about not getting paid, very worried about that. He felt that he was doing all the work because Sugrue didn't know too much about staging a major fight. And it didn't matter to Hal whether he was talking to a king or whoever, he didn't like to take shit from anybody.'

Schulberg was domiciled at the Gresham Hotel. From the moment Conrad had booked his suite there, the Gresham became the focal point of the scene that surrounds every big fight. The majority of the visiting press, the various denizens of the boxing world and every other hanger-on with enough money or clout to mix it could be found in the lobby or the bar of the hotel that week. No matter what part of the world Ali went to, an eclectic cast of characters would magically appear during the build-up and lend a particular atmosphere. As Steve Eisner, the lone member of the Lewis party to be staying there, discovered, the Gresham had a distinctive flavour all its own.

'Don Elbaum turns up at my door one night and insists I come downstairs to the bar to meet some fine Irishmen,' says Eisner. 'I go down, and sitting in this oak-panelled booth with Don was Jack McKinney, a tabloid guy from the *Philadelphia Daily News*, and this other Irish guy. The Irish guy is talking a lot and drinking a lot and the drunker he gets the better he gets. Eventually, I ask him: "What do you do?" And at this stage, the guy is crocked, but he says: "I'm the master bombmaker for the IRA!" "Bullshit!" I say. He opens up his coat and he's got gelignite and dynamite caps in his vest. "Don't worry, lads," he says laughing, "they'd not dare shoot me." I got the hell out of there quick.'

Similar scenes were being replicated all over the hotel and those in the inner circle got to go upstairs to Conrad's rooms on the top floor. At the age of 87, Budd Schulberg's memory of that week nearly thirty years ago isn't quite as detailed or graphic as it used to be. He directs me towards something he wrote in the past. Back in 1982, his recall when penning the introduction to Conrad's memoir was, predictably, more comprehensive.

'In a lavish suite, the Conrad's held court over that deliciously mixed company they knew how to attract,' wrote Schulberg. 'There was the old gallant, John Huston, up from his horsey estate in Galway. Stars from the Abbey Theatre filled the room with beautiful talk. Gun-runners for the IRA were, Hal found out later, literally making deals in the bedroom. Peter O'Toole was there, and three choir-boy killers for the Provisionals, incredibly casual about a night of terror they had survived in Belfast. There were two former light-heavyweight champions, Jose Torres, now writing for the *Village Voice*, and Billy Conn, a cynical Irish-American who had extended Joe Louis in his prime, and who was now complaining loudly of the dullness of his ancestors' motherland.'

For a promoter seeking a celebrity with a boxing pedigree to assist with the publicity, Conn must have looked like the dream ticket. His mother, Maggie McFarland, had come across to America in steerage from Queenstown (now Cobh) in County Cork while still a young girl and never lost the accent. When Billy Conn Sr gave his son a pair of boxing gloves one particular Christmas in Pittsburgh, Maggie manufactured a pair of green shorts to complement them, and even as a pro, Conn fought with a shamrock emblazoned on his shorts.

Thirty-one years after his first epic with Louis had ensured his place in boxing folklore, Conrad rang him up and offered him $500 and all his expenses paid. That he'd never been to Ireland before was enough to persuade him to make the trip. Unfortunately, Conn had a distinctive take on his ancestry. When asked to explain why he foolishly chose to mix it with Louis in the thirteenth round of a fight he was so clearly winning, and in so doing ended up being counted out with two seconds remaining in that round, he loved to answer: 'What's the use of being Irish if you can't be thick?' Despite this cavalier attitude to his heritage, Conn said later that he signed more autographs that week in Dublin than any other time in his life.

'I remember my father telling us that the Gresham was the best place to be in Dublin,' says Ryan Conn. 'Ulick O'Connor, the writer, and my father were drinking in the Gresham bar one night and I guess there were a few guys in there with IRA connections. My father started to bawl them out saying things like: "You guys have to be crazy. We get along with Protestants. We don't care what they are. We don't worry about whether somebody's a Catholic or a Protestant in Pittsburgh. Forget about that stuff, we don't bother anybody just because they are Protestant!" He started to tell them off like that and they took it kind of hard. So eventually they got mad and I think they decided we better take this guy for a ride until Ulick O'Connor went over to them and said: "Don't pay any attention to him, he doesn't know what he's talking about." O'Connor seemed to be quite famous there, everybody knew who he was so that got my father off the hook.

'My father was the type of person who always said what he thought. A few of the Irish newspaper guys asked him on another occasion: 'Well, Billy, you finally saw your homeland, the country of your ancestors, what are your impressions of Ireland and of Dublin?" What do you think he said? "All I can say is I'm sure glad my mother didn't miss the boat all those years ago!" When Ulick O'Connor got mad at him and reminded him that he was being paid to say nice things, my father said: "I don't care, they're a hundred years behind the times here." Of course, he told us afterwards that he had a great time and really liked the place but he just felt like making a controversial comment.'

If the literary and pugilistic set were enjoying themselves to the full, Ali wasn't shirking from the task of selling the fight. Every morning, there was a different eye-catching photograph of him in the newspapers. Whether it was jawing with Jack Lynch, swinging a hurley with Eddie Keher, jogging in the Dublin mountains or pretending to be arrested by a couple of uniformed Gardai, he was doing his bit to keep the column inches coming. Before, during and after the public sparring sessions, he didn't stint either. Everybody who made it into the handball alley left with a story or two.

'He was always on duty, always on the stage,' says Barney Eastwood. 'He'd come into the gym, smile and make funny remarks. One day, he came over to where I was standing and asked: "Who's this man here? Is this man in the fight game?" "Yeah," somebody said, "he's a promoter from Northern Ireland." So with that, he walks over to me and whispers in my ear: "The smartest warrior doesn't have to fight." That was one thing that stuck with me, I felt that was clever. Another day, there was a boy of fourteen or fifteen years of age in the gym, and somebody was talking about the boy refusing to go to school. They were saying that this was a smart kid who was wasting his life because he wouldn't stay in school. Now, Ali wasn't even in the conversation. He was lacing up his boots or putting on his jacket while this guy was complaining about the young lad. Ali got up, bounced around a couple of times, went over towards the boy and said: "Always remember, young man, without knowledge, you're less than everybody." The boy just looked at him. The last thing he expected was Ali to come over to him and say something. But the guy had some great sayings.'

Of course, whenever he spotted journalists carrying notebooks and pens, Ali cranked the performance up a gear. After one sparring session, when the inquisitors inevitably got around to the topic of Frazier, he delivered the usual quota of put-downs and criticisms of the new champion. However, Tom Cryan, a journalist with the *Irish Independent*, pushed the envelope a little further by asking Ali: 'Did you try to prove something to yourself when you fought Frazier?'

This was the cue he needed. Ali jumped to his feet in order to better deliver a speech the passion of which was accentuated by him repeatedly jabbing the air around Cryan's face. As his fists seemed to be getting nearer his questioner's nose, the reporter decided that discretion might be the better part of valour.

'Sceptical of his ability to judge it to a fraction as he went "pow, pow",' wrote Cryan of the incident, 'all the time ranting about what he would do to Joe Frazier, I performed what onlookers described as my most athletic exercise for years, when skipping off a table to the safety of a corridor outside a packed dressing room.'

Everybody departed with an anecdote all their own. Eleven years old, Gerry Thornley was brought along to see Ali work out by his father David, a politician and a boxing fanatic.

'The old man got us into the dressing room afterwards,' says Thornley, now the rugby correspondent of the *Irish Times*. 'Ali was there with his entourage and I was wearing a T-shirt that one of his entourage guys commented on and they were all laughing about this. Then Ali sort of stood over me and started a sequence where he was jabbing either side of my ear. I just stood and froze. He tried to engage me in conversation but I was so overawed – this was like meeting God – that I couldn't speak. He was like something carved out of stone looking down on me as he threw these jabs. This was Muhammad Ali and I couldn't say boo to him. I don't think I actually said one single word. Embarrassed, I just thrust out my autograph book and he signed it with a flourish – *from Muhammad Ali* – and then his mates made some jokes and that was pretty much it. To my regret, I never actually managed to open my mouth and speak to him.'

Few, if any, sports people have ever been as conscious of their role as a public figure as Ali, and in Dublin, he fulfilled all the preconceived notions people had about him. They expected him to be gregarious and open and charming, and for the most part, he was. There were other dimensions to his persona which served to enhance his image even further. For participating in a photo shoot with Pat Quinn, proprietor of the Quinnsworth supermarket chain, Ali was paid £500. After consulting with Angelo Dundee, it was decided that his fee was to be donated to St Raphael's School for mentally handicapped children in Celbridge, County Kildare.

'We were delighted with the contribution,' says Bill Shorten, a manager in St Raphael's at that time. 'We had just built the school and we were in the process of raising money to construct a swimming pool. Money was very scarce in those days and the state would only give you a grant if you raised a certain portion yourself through garden fêtes and whatever else you could muster. Myself and Mary Walsh, the secretary of the school's "parents and friends" fund-raising committee, went out to Opperman's to meet Ali and have our photograph taken with him and Pat Quinn. He was exceptionally nice to us, his eyes almost spoke to you they were so impish and warm and friendly. He put us at our ease instantly, but at the same time he was always bouncing on his toes as he spoke. You felt like you were in the ring with him the way he kept bouncing on his toes. You have to understand that was a very substantial donation for us at that time. To give you an idea of how much money that was, I

The Big Fight: Ali conquers Ireland, while a posse of Gardai tries to keep him from being engulfed by adoring fans. (Ali's trainer Angelo Dundee is to the Greatest's left.)

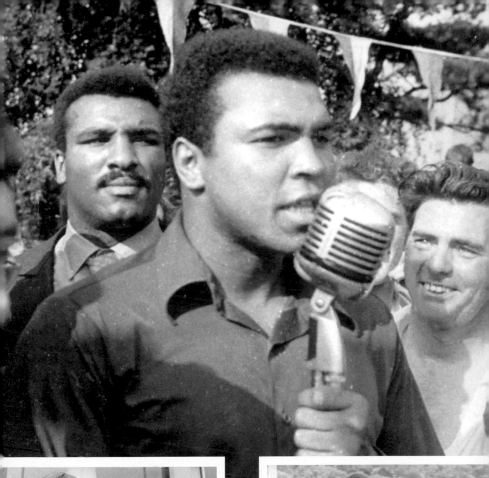

(*Main picture*) Ali addresses a crowd
as his brother Rahaman keeps a
watchful eye on proceedings.
(*Above left*) Eye of the tiger: one fan
feels the wrath of the champ.
(*Right*) Rahaman Ali finds his
signature in demand.

Hurl away: *Irish Independent* journalist Raymond Smith (*top left picture, next to Ali*) mediates as legendary Kilkenny hurler Eddie Keher shows Ali the beauty of the fastest field game in the world.

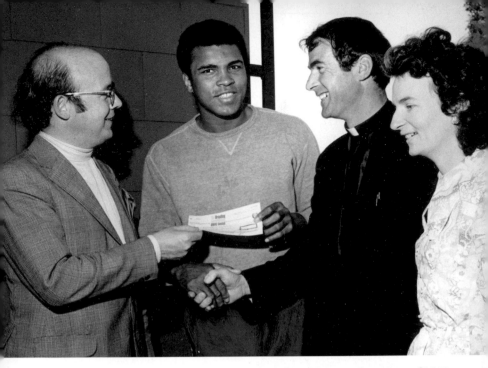

Supermarket tycoon Pat Quinn and Ali hand over a donation of £500 to Brother Camillus (Bill Shorten) and Mary Walsh of St Raphael's School for the Mentally Handicapped in Celbridge.

I am the prettiest! Ali entertains some female admirers.

Taoiseach Jack Lynch (*right*) imparts words of wisdom at Leinster House
as Ali and Butty Sugrue (*second from right*) listen intently.

Sharp-dressed man: Harold Conrad turning on the charm at a press conference.

I'll whup him now! Ali shows another use for his shillelagh.

Ali working the speedball inside the handball alley at Croke Park.

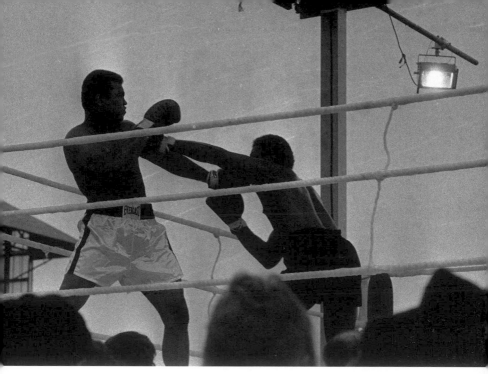

Let's get it on: Ali tries to keep Al 'Blue' Lewis at arm's length.

Cornered: Lewis adopts a defensive pose as Ali launches one more barrage.

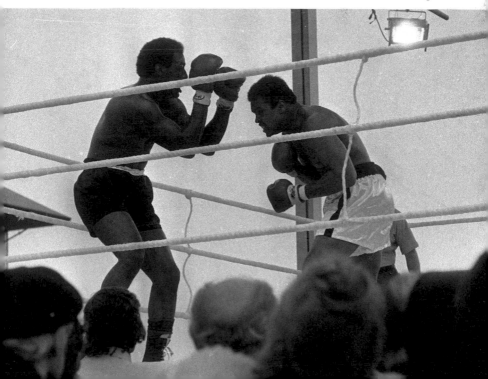

The end is near:
Lewis feels the back
of Ali's right hand.

remember hiring a teacher in the school two years later on a wage of £18 per week.'

Quinnsworth got an excellent return from their part in the deal too. Under the slogan, 'We are the Champions', they ran a newspaper campaign advertising select product prices: a six-pack of Bass cost 45p, a giant-size box of Kellogg's Corn Flakes was 10p and a bottle of Goodall's Salad Cream went for 14p. Beneath the picture of Quinn and Ali were both men's autographs and the following uninspired manifesto:

> Like Muhammad Ali, Quinnsworth are the Champions! Our stores are the prettiest, our value undefeated. Our managers are real pros in the price-fight game. You meet lots of contenders for the title of Supermarket Champions but we whup 'em every time! Conceited? No, we're not conceited . . . we're convinced!'

Quinnsworth distributed free photographs of Ali and Quinn at their checkouts until stocks ran out. In a city where black faces were still rare enough to draw second and even third glances, the most famous African-American in the world was suddenly everywhere, and sightings of him engulfed by hordes of white children and adults became commonplace. It wasn't unusual for him to walk down O'Connell Street, bringing the traffic to a stop as he did his Pied Piper impression.

'One thing that amazed me was the way the local people adored Ali,' says Budd Schulberg. 'At times, I thought the adulation was very much the same as if he was walking through Harlem or some place back home. Wherever he went, the crowd would follow him, fall in behind and start to chant: "Ali, Ali, Ali." They'd be everywhere all around him. He had an amazing effect on them. Much more than I expected really. They loved him more than I would have expected, they were really crazy about him. He was very much the same Ali as usual except he didn't know quite what he was getting into and he was really pleased with the way everybody responded to him everywhere he went.

He was very funny with it. The sense of humour the Irish have, I think he related very well to that. He was very much the same going down the street, stopping and talking to everybody, just like I'd seen him do before in places like Atlanta. He was really enjoying himself.'

In hindsight, Jose Torres believes that the warmth and adulation Ali received in Ireland back then had a more profound and lasting effect on the fighter.

'The reception was amazing,' says Torres. 'Now, I want to tell you something. I think that experience reminded him of the goodness of white people and he began easing his attacks on the white man because of experiences like that. It was after that when he began to take out of his dictionary all the talk about the white devils. How could he think bad of white people when he had all these white people loving him like that in Dublin?'

Even though the newspapers were full of stories about him residing at Opperman's, the public's appetite for Ali meant that a crowd always kept vigil outside the entrance to the Gresham Hotel, the people figuring he'd have to pass through there at some stage each day.

'The atmosphere around town was electric,' says John McCormack. 'You'd see groups of people standing outside hotels and pubs saying: "We're down here because we're going to see Muhammad Ali coming out here tonight." They'd wait for hours and hours but he'd be gone the other way if he was ever there at all. All the pubs around the Gresham were waiting and waiting in the hope that he'd come in but he didn't. And you know the way Dublin people are, some fella would come in and say: "He's supposed to be coming in the minute." So they'd sit there for hours waiting and waiting.'

The public's seemingly insatiable appetite for all things related to Ali wasn't translating into ticket sales. Not even Sugrue's announcement that any profits from the event would be donated to charity had a noticeable effect on demand. The advertisements booked for that week's papers had the line *Proceeds to the Greatest Cause Known to Man: The Mentally*

86

Handicapped Children tagged on in a last-ditch effort to appeal to people's consciences. Sugrue also enlisted the help of a bishop who gave the fight a plug during Mass that Sunday, informing the congregation that since such a worthy charity would benefit, the bout was worth supporting. None of this was enough to placate Conrad. Experience taught him that if the tickets weren't going well with just three days to go before the fight, the promotion was heading for certain trouble.

By that Sunday, almost all the 3,000 ringside seats had been snapped up for £15 apiece, but there was room inside Croke Park for another 50,000, and the stand tickets were not going well. Conrad later claimed that he tried to make Sugrue aware early of how much financial bother they could be in, only to have the Kerryman dismiss the fears with talk of an inevitably large walk-up crowd on the night. Conrad warned him that the handicapped children would be lucky to receive a Tootsie Roll (an American candy bar) unless there was a rapid increase in sales. In private, the New Yorker also came to the conclusion that those people who loitered in hotel lobbies for hours to see Ali in the flesh were happy enough to catch a glimpse of their hero, and thereafter not bothered about actually seeing him fight.

Despite the bishop's words from the altar, the omens were not good as the clock began to tick down, with 17 July, in particular, proving something of a Black Monday for the promoters. When Ali failed to turn up for sparring at Croke Park that afternoon, the disgruntled crowd began to voice their discontent by slow handclapping before angrily demanding their money back. The Gardai had to be called to control and then disperse the unhappy punters. Conrad's day wasn't improving, however. One reporter approached him with the news that word on the street was the fight had already sold out. All his experience in the publicity game hadn't prepared him for the way a good rumour could sweep through a place like Dublin.

'You don't even need to have purchased your ticket in advance, though naturally we would like as much advance selling as possible,' he told reporters. 'Money will be taken at the turnstiles just as for a hurling or football game at the venue. Remember that Croke Park is a very big place as boxing venues go. And it takes a lot of filling. I do not know how rumours have begun to circulate in the city that the tickets are sold out for the fight. I want to scotch those rumours emphatically.'

While all this was playing out, Ali was tucked up in his hotel bed, fighting an infection.

'I wasn't hiding anything, I just didn't want people to know,' says Angelo Dundee, with a trainer's finely tuned grasp of doublespeak. 'He was battling against a cold and I tried to keep it low key. I wanted to protect him so I had a doctor coming in to give him a penicillin shot. Don't you know, we were in the room and there were a couple of newspapermen outside the room, so I had the doctor going in and out a different way to give him the shot. So Ali comes out afterwards as I'm talking to the newspaper guys and says: "Wait a minute, do you know I'm getting these shots because I have a cold!" He told all and sundry. I was trying to keep it quiet so the fans wouldn't get worried and the promoters wouldn't get worried. It was no more than a sniffle really, but for me a sniffle is a sign that I need to step in and take protective steps, to make sure it doesn't get worse.'

Even before the illness, Dundee had become concerned that Ali had too many extra-curricular engagements booked too close to the fight. How could he possibly prepare to beat Lewis when every appointment Ali fulfilled evolved into at least a two-hour spectacular?

'I have heard press reports refer to that particular malaise as "a mere sniffle",' wrote Paddy Monaghan. 'They knew nothing. But I did and I can swear now that it was a very heavy head cold. The camp was content to allow people to believe that it was of little importance but Muhammad was feeling pretty rough. In the meantime, there was much toing and froing going on around Ali, what with the press, the celebrities, the sports, the well-wishers, the lot! All wanting him to be here, there and everywhere. Nobody at all seemed to have any consideration for the man himself. Angelo had a full-time job on his hands just seeing to it that Muhammad got as much rest as possible.'

Of course, Dundee confining him to quarters for much of Monday wasn't going to work either. Despite the fact that part of the reason he was resting up was so he could honour a prior commitment to a do a lengthy television interview that night, Ali quickly grew bored with his bed and decided to hold a press conference in his room. The reporters trooped in to find him with his head propped up on a pillow and his brother Rahaman beside him. When it appeared his star might finally be falling, he unfurled the sort of down-home anecdote guaranteed to counter any negative public reaction to him disappointing the multitudes at Croke Park that afternoon.

'Travelling's an experience for afterwards,' said Ali, with the sheets pulled up almost to his neck. 'Like you don't appreciate countries like this 'til you go home – the culture, the people, the way they talk, the quietness. Then you go back home, the smog, the rat race, the noise – then you appreciate it. Oh, Man! This is the first European country I've been received and welcomed in by heads of state – genuine, not just acting. We went out walking around here on Sunday night and this old lady asked us in for a cup of tea. You know, we stayed there a long time. It was her home – and we drank cups of tea with Irish bread and jam and cake – Oh, Man!'

7

In Living Colour

On Monday evening, Ali and a few senior members of his retinue decamped to the RTE television studios in Donnybrook to record an extended interview with journalist Cathal O'Shannon. To be shown on Tuesday night at ten forty-five, immediately after an experimental colour broadcast of 'Show-jumping from London', the promoters were fervently hoping it might have a positive impact on the size of Wednesday's walk-up crowd. Upon arriving, Ali's first port of call was the make-up department. Far from the cameras, he was already on the stage. Settling into the chair to be prepared for the spotlight by make-up lady Evelyn Lunny, he couldn't resist a warm-up performance before the main event.

'I took out my powder and started powdering him, holding my knees together to stop me falling,' says Lunny. 'And he turned to everybody in the place and he said: "Isn't this just the prettiest face you've ever put powder on?" I was only in make-up about a year and I was very, very excited. Truly, I had never made up anybody who was coloured – Indian, Chinese or Black – up to that point. So I thought, what have we got in the department, and to be honest, we didn't have a lot. We had make-up to make white people look black or various shades. Then he turned around to everybody again and says: "Look, she thinks she's going to hurt me with a powder puff and I'm about to face Al 'Blue' Lewis!"'

It was a face that didn't need much enhancement.

The idea for the television programme came from John Condon, a director at RTE who realised that it wasn't too often that one of the world's most famous people hung around town for more than a week. He asked O'Shannon to get involved in the project even though the journalist knew very little about sport. What he lacked in specialist knowledge, O'Shannon made up for with interview technique and exhaustive research. As soon as he knew there was a chance he'd be sitting down with Ali, he read every article and book he could unearth. The extent of his homework comes through and three decades later 'Muhammad Ali versus Cathal O'Shannon' remains a classic encounter. Getting Ali into the chair, however, wasn't without its little dramas.

'We went up to Opperman's place to meet him,' says O'Shannon. 'He'd already been there for two or three days and it seemed to me that every whore in Ireland had turned up there, including black whores from Manchester and London. God knows how they all got in. Within an hour of us arriving at the hotel, his mother arrived and she had with him his infant child Muhammad Junior. When she saw all these black whores, she chased them all out of it and then she gave out yards to him. She gave out stink and we all witnessed this right in front of the check-in desk. She followed him around the place, shouting "Get rid of these bitches" and all sorts. Anyway, they were cleared out and he looked very sheepish at this time. Rahaman, a very smooth-looking fella with a little moustache who reminded me a lot of a black Errol Flynn, cooled the mother down. In the midst of all this stuff, we chatted to Ali for a few minutes about the possibility of an interview, and he said: "Yeah, I'll do it."

'The question was what would we pay him? We knew that he had been to the BBC a year before and done a Michael Parkinson interview and they had flown over about twenty of his people with him especially and had to pay him 14,000 quid. We paid him one hundred pounds. A hundred pounds, imagine that, Christ almighty, you'd be amazed at the difficulty we had with that. When Angelo Dundee said he wanted the money in cash on the night, we had to go into the canteen in RTE to try and find cash because we had a cheque written. I haven't a clue why they wanted cash.'

The search for used notes in the cash registers of the canteen wasn't even the worst part of the build-up. That happened inside the VIP room moments before taping began.

'The first thing Ali said to me in RTE was "I hate this fucking place!"' says O'Shannon. 'I thought, this is great, we're going on in twenty minutes to tape an hour-and-a-half programme. So I said: "How could you say that? You've only just got here." He said: "No, no, I mean the place I'm staying in." He hated Opperman's because the previous night he had come into town, walked along O'Connell Street, gone into the Gresham Hotel, and of course he was followed by every kid and hanger-on walking around O'Connell Street. He loved the crowd, adored it actually and loved showing off, so he felt too isolated out in Opperman's. To be honest, I nearly crapped myself when he said: "I hate this fucking place!"'

By the time O'Shannon was under the lights in the studio that normally housed the station's flagship programme, *The Late Late Show*, he had regained his professional demeanour. Apart from Dundee, Harold Conrad and a couple of others sitting in the front row, he and Condon had filled the seats by inviting family and friends, all of whom were suitably thrilled at the chance to spend an evening in Ali's company. Many of the exchanges are typical Ali at that time in his life, well-worn lines freshly delivered to a new and receptive audience. From the moment he strode across the stage in an open-necked shirt and a pair of slacks, he had them eating out of his hand. Settling back into the chair, he crossed his legs at the ankles and grew ever so slightly embarrassed when O'Shannon opened with a question to the audience.

O'SHANNON: Well, do you think he's the prettiest?

ALI (*shaking his head*): I didn't say that, I don't know how that got out.

That was to be his last pretence of modesty for the duration.

O'SHANNON: You are doing a lot of fighting?

ALI: Well, yes, I think the boxing game should stay alive, I think every contender should get a shot at the title. The new tramp, I mean champ, Joe Frazier is not doing nothing, fighting once every seven months, fighting people you could beat and you can't fight.

O'SHANNON: You're so right about that.

ALI: I have to keep the game alive.

O'SHANNON: How do you feel about the fight with Al 'Blue' Lewis?

ALI: I'm fighting Lewis for one reason, mainly because Frazier won't fight him, George Foreman won't fight him and Jerry Quarry won't fight him. To most boxers and managers, this is just a business and they figure they got a top contender and they don't want to take a chance and lose unless they are paid great. Top-notch fighters fighting 'Blue' Lewis can't receive a proper payment because he's not famous and yet he has a chance of beating them. They have nothing to gain and everything to lose. I'm fighting him because everyone else is ducking him and he's a good fighter. Plus, it would be kinda hard to bring a top-notch fighter here because the price couldn't be put up.

O'SHANNON: What sort of a chance does he have with you?

ALI: Two chances . . . (*Pauses for effect.*)

O'SHANNON: What are they?

ALI: Slim and none (*He bows his head and puckers up his lips, satisfied with the gag.*)

O'SHANNON: I suppose I asked for that . . . Angelo Dundee has just handed me a piece of paper saying you hope to go to fight in Tehran in three weeks' time.

ALI: I – Ran in Tehran. Yes, we're going, just an exhibition, a government invitation. We're working on it now.

O'SHANNON: So your next big fight, I suppose, is against Floyd Patterson.

ALI: Patterson, right, the rabbit.

O'SHANNON: The rabbit?

ALI: I call him the rabbit.

O'SHANNON: Why's that?

ALI: The way he fights and he calls me Clay and my name is now Muhammad Ali but he insists on Clay so I call him the rabbit. Plus, I'm going to fight the rabbit in the garden.

O'SHANNON: Madison Square Garden, of course . . . You then go on to fight Frazier, I gather?

ALI: Yes, if he comes out of hiding. He bought a plantation down in South Carolina, some chicken plantation. I know he's a slave but he don't have to buy no plantation.

O'SHANNON: How do you really feel about him?

ALI: Well, he's a good slugger. He's not scientific. He's rough. Physically, I know I beat him. I won nine rounds. He's already ugly and I beat him so bad that night and he was so ugly that his face should have been donated to the bureau of wildlife. (*The most over-used line of the trip receives yet another airing and the crowd erupts.*)

O'SHANNON: He toured here with a show.

ALI: I heard. He flopped like he do everywhere else. He's got a singing group called the Knockouts and he thought just because they gave him my title he could go everywhere and draw people and get rich. I understand he draws eighty people or maybe a hundred people in a 20,000-seat arena. In London, in a 4,000-seat arena he drew twelve people and had the nerve to keep on with the show.

O'SHANNON: He did a little better here, he got eighty-seven at one actually and 1,041 at another.

ALI: I know I can beat him singing but I don't call myself a singer. I can come here and fill every place because the people know who the real champ is.

O'SHANNON: But you have been a singer too, you had a show called *Buck White*, didn't you?

ALI: I was in a play called *Big Time Buck White*, a black militant play about the problems we have in America. The play was a flop but I was a hit. The play lasted six days but the worst critics said my part was a hit. I want to get that straight.

O'SHANNON: Why is it you think that you draw the crowds? Of all the sportsmen in the world, you are a great crowd drawer.

ALI: Mainly personality has a lot to do with it. Like a salesman's business depends entirely on his personality. If he's rude and unsympathetic, the buyer will hope that he goes away and never comes back. But very often if the salesman is good he can make a person buy something he doesn't even intend to . . . Very few fighters, if you take the camera up close and see my nose and my face, I'm not ugly, I'm not ugly like most fighters. They've got noses like that (*presses in on the nose*) and ears like that (*pulls left ear forward*). 'How you feeling, champ?' 'Ugh, ugh, ugh . . .' I'm pretty, I'm a pretty fighter and I have a personality. I know how to talk to the wise heads. I had a talk with your great Mr Lynch in your parliament house and I know how to talk to men like you with less intelligence than myself . . .

There is a prolonged bout of laughter then that causes him to grow especially animated

. . . Just listen to the people laugh, just listen to them laugh. Very few comedians can do this and that's their job. It's personality that attracts. Like in America I stand up for black people and, regardless of what it costs me, I speak out for what I believe in. Just like in Ireland you got people fighting for what they believe. Then you have all the Muslims in Pakistan, Saudi Arabia, Syria, Lebanon, India, Abu Dhabi, all throughout Libya, Kuwait, they all recognise me and call the name Muhammad Ali. You add all of this up and all I represent and I AM THE GREATEST! (*Slapping the chair with his hands, his voice is at full pitch.*) I CANNOT LOSE! I'M PRETTY! Many want to say this but they fear it. They see this in myself and some hate me for it and some love me for it and add it all up and we got a large crowd. Joe Frazier is ugly. He's flat-footed, he can't sing, he can't fight and he has no personality.

O'SHANNON: He can't fight?

ALI: No, he's a slugger, a street fighter. Don't get me wrong. He's good but he's not skilful. He's known for taking a lot of punches. He's not like Floyd Patterson or Sugar Ray Robinson or Joe Louis or Jack Johnson or Jack Dempsey. These were great scientific fighters. Joe Frazier will take five punches to hit you once.

O'SHANNON: Why do you think he beat you the last time?

ALI: The reason he got the decision if you looked at my face and his face after the fight, both his eyes were closed, his lip was cut, his nose was bloodied, his head was swollen and he spent one month in the hospital. Did you all hear that? He spent thirty days in intensive care, no phone calls and no visitors. That's a terrible beating when you have to stay rested for thirty days. I'm not complaining. He got the decision but next time I'll get him. I played too much with him, plus I found out that three of the judges was on the local draft board.

With characteristic modesty, O'Shannon downplays in his part in the success of the show, feeling it was the kind of thing Ali had done 'a thousand times before'.

'It's strange but, you know, with Ali, there was no way you could go wrong from an interviewer's point of view,' says O'Shannon. 'You knew he would react properly because he was such a bloody showman. A total and absolute pro. If I had dropped myself in it, I felt he would have picked me up out of it. I was in the safest possible hands. I'd worked out the questions but didn't even go over them with him. I just said we're going to cover this sort of area and that was enough. I had interviewed John F. Kennedy before that but to tell you the God's honest truth, this was a much bigger thing.'

There are certain occasions in the interview when astute questions play a vital role in provoking the subject and offering a glimpse of something more substantive than his practised put-downs of Frazier and pre-cooked punchlines.

O'SHANNON: How was it, Muhammad, anyway to be a Negro boy in the South?

ALI: We say black now.

O'SHANNON: All right, black. Is it not the same thing?

ALI: No, Negro is . . . we're talking about . . . all people are named after a country. The Chinese are named after China, the Cubans are named after Cuba, Irish people are named after Ireland, Indonesians named after Indonesia, Japanese are named after Japan, Australians are named after Australia, but there's no country named Negro!

O'SHANNON: All right, let me . . .

ALI: Do you understand?

O'SHANNON: I understand.

ALI: You're not as dumb as you look.

O'SHANNON: Do I look that dumb?

ALI: Naah, only kidding.

O'SHANNON: What I really mean is did you feel that you were deprived, that you and your family and other blacks were second-class citizens?

ALI: Did we feel it? We knew it! Not only second class! Add up all of the nationalities you have on earth – they come first. Right now, you can come to my home town and you're freer in America than I am. The Chinese, the Japanese that the black people helped America to fight or even the Germans are freer. The day after the war in Vietnam, the Vietcong will be more of a citizen than the American Negro. So we might be the fiftieth of sixtieth class if you break it down. If we were just second class we'd be all right.

O'SHANNON: This is something you feel strongly about?

ALI: Strongly? I know it's the truth, I live right there every day.

O'SHANNON: What attracted you to Islam in the first instance?

ALI: The Muslim religion is the true teachings of Elijah Muhammad right there in America and no power structure or nobody will challenge him. It is the history of ourselves, the history of our true religion, our nationality and our names. We don't have our names. I notice how proud you all are of your names. Chinese have names like Ching Chung, Lu Chin. Russians have names like Kosygin or Khrushchev. And you have names like O'Connor and Grady and Kennedy. [*How interesting that he should refer to the surname that crops up in his own family?*] Africans have names like Lomumba Nkroma. Jews have names like Weinstein and Goldberg. Italians got names like Dundee, Bienvenuti and Marciano. We have names like Grady [*one more reference to his ancestors*] and Clay and Hawkins and Smith and Jones and Johnson but we're black.

O'SHANNON: These are the slave names?

ALI: When I heard this I knew it was the truth because it's history. Muhammad Ali is a beautiful black name, name of our ancestors. When I heard this I just had to walk out of the Church of Christianity because they never taught us our true knowledge. Then they told me how we were brainwashed in America. We see Jesus, he's white with blond hair and blue eyes . . . We see the Lord's Supper, all white people . . . We see the angels in heaven, all white people. We look at Miss Universe, a white woman . . . Miss America, a white woman . . . Miss World, a white woman . . . Even Tarzan, the King of the Jungles in Africa, he was white. (*The audience find this so funny that obviously enthused by their reaction, he puts his hands over his mouth in the manner of Johnny Weissmuller's Tarzan.*) You see a white man swinging around Africa, ahhhhhyaaayaaaa, with a diaper on, ahhhyaaayaaaa . . . he beats up all the Africans and breaks the lion's jaw. The Africans been in Africa for centuries but can't yet talk to the animals! But Tarzan, all of a sudden some goat raised him up and he can talk to the animals. So I'm just showing you how the black man in America has been whitewashed in his mind. And then we look at the good cowboys, they rode the white horses . . . and the President lives in a white house. They got TV commercials for White House cigars, White Swan soap, King White soap, White tissue paper, White Rain hair rinse, White Tornado floor wax, White Plus toothpaste. The Angel fruit cake was the white cake but the devil fruit cake was the chocolate cake. Everything good is white! Our religion teaches us the knowledge of ourselves, the knowledge of our culture, the knowledge of our history. It makes us want to be with our own, marry our own, live with our own, clean up ourselves, do for ourselves, quit forcing ourselves on white neighbourhoods, clean up our own neighbourhoods, makes us proud and makes us identify with our own brothers around the world. Being an intelligent man, I'm not only winning in boxing or in my stand on the draft, I'm a winner also in the movement that I follow for my people whose leader is Elijah Muhammad who we believe was taught by Allah, God himself, to teach the so-called American Negro the truth that's been hidden from them for four hundred years, the truth which will free them!

O'SHANNON: Why is it do you think the black Muslims preach the separation of the races, rather than integration of the races, as indeed many American blacks do?

ALI: Well, when we say separation, we know that as of now, we always have to be trading with one another, living with one another. When we say separate, we mean mentally, mainly. We've tried integrating for four hundred years and we been kicked and shot and brutalised. I understand this is some of your problem in Ireland where people are tired of being dominated by certain groups, tired of being rude and being mean, and they want to do for themselves. The same way in all countries – people are just tired and they're revolutionising things. They want to be free. We been in America under white domination, lynched, killed, raped, castrated, shot down daily. No justice in the courts, deprived of freedom, justice and equality and we now just want to be free. We can't do it. We've found out that black and white are disagreeable in peace. They can't get along together so we think we should just now quit fighting, quit being violent now that we're doctors, lawyers and mechanics, now that we're educated and we don't need to pick cotton any more. We got millions of blacks being born in hospitals every day and there are no jobs. We think that we should now go on some land and build and construct and do for ourselves, that's all.

O'SHANNON: Do you mean in actual fact that there should be separate parts of the United States only for Negroes and only for whites?

ALI: The holy Elijah Muhammad teaches us that we've been there four hundred years. We fought the Japanese, we fought the Germans, we fought the Koreans. If America went to war with Ireland tomorrow, the black people would be over here so fast shooting you. All the black people would be over here shooting you with the American flag. And we believe that since we been fighting all of America's enemies, not our enemies, we've worked four hundred years, sixteen hours a day, from sun up to sun down, that we should now be repaid. Don't give us nothing but repay us. You got fifty states and we make up 10 per cent of the population. Then divide up 10 per cent of the land and let us build our own stores, grow our own food, make our own suits, be like other people, not always begging white people for houses, begging for jobs, begging for a seat in your restaurant. May I use your toilet? May I ride on your bus? Now that I'm grown and educated and now we're no longer slaves and we can't get along, just let me go and live by myself like other people. There ain't nothing wrong with that.

O'SHANNON: Muslims don't believe in war. You certainly don't and you demonstrated that by refusing to join the American Army, but you've said on one occasion that you could believe in a holy war.

ALI: The holy Koran teaches us that we declare ourselves righteous Muslims who take no part in wars, no way, fashion or form, that take the lives of humans unless it's a holy war declared by God, Allah himself. This hasn't happened. If it do happen, we have a way of knowing because our religious leaders speak out. But we don't take no part in wars, not just the Vietnam War, no war.

O'SHANNON: Would you fight in a holy war, a war of this sort? How would you know that you should fight?

ALI: That's what I'm trying to say. We have a leader who will speak, all countries have leaders, we have a leader. If we are attacked, and we are right, we believe in fighting, but not being the aggressor.

O'SHANNON: Elijah Muhammad has said something that perhaps us white people have misunderstood, perhaps you can explain it to me, he said: 'White men are devils.'

ALI: Yes, he means just what he says. The deeds and the works of the man, what the American devils did to us. All the lynching, the killing, cutting the black people's privates out and sticking it in the mouth. I got a book called *The Hundred Years of Lynching* written by a white man. They did this for years. They took black women who were four months pregnant, hung us up by the feet, stuck a dagger in the stomach and ripped it just to pull the unborn baby out. Just to put fear in other slaves. They tied up black people to two horses and two horses pulled their arms and legs out. Lemonade trains with white people and white children of America used to come and watch them tie up ten or fifteen black men and pour gasoline on them and watch them burn alive. They took us and hung us up on trees and shot us. They cut our heads off, took the legs off and gave them to little boys. This is worse than the devil. The preacher in the church told us that the devil was under the ground and he'd wait 'til we died before he'd burn us up. This white devil in America burned us while we was alive. He didn't wait 'til we died. What I'm trying to say is the deeds and the works. If Elijah Muhammad can stand up in America for forty-two years before my little black self was born and say that the American white man is the devil, then the white man should get up and say: 'You are a liar!' and carry him to court and say: 'We are not the devil.' Not one American, not one government official, not one mayor, not one senator, none of them will stand up and say they are not devils and this man is lying. What am I to do? I believe it.

Throughout this speech, he had the index finger on his right hand at full extension, wagging it determinedly as he spoke the last line. Keeping a serious scowl on his face, he glared at the audience with his arms wide in exasperation. To his credit, O'Shannon didn't allow him to get away with such a widespread condemnation of an entire race.

O'SHANNON: Do you believe that every white man is the devil? Angelo Dundee? Harold Conrad?

ALI: Angelo Dundee is Italian, he's got a lot of black blood in him. (*Pause for laughter.*) And Harold Conrad is a Jew. What I'm saying to you is this (*staring into the camera*): Elijah Muhammad, our leader, teaches us this and I believe everything he says. It's not for me to prove. You must remember this. You have not lynched me. It wasn't the Germans who did this to us, it wasn't the white Canadians who was right on our border. He's putting the emphasis on the American devils. Let's say we got one white fella in America who has proved that he means right. Let's say that we got another one – white people have died in demonstrations for black people – now here's the position I'm in. Let's say ten thousand rattlesnakes coming to bite me and in that ten thousand, there was one thousand who didn't mean no harm, and I knew there was a good thousand snakes out there. They all look alike so what should I do? Keep the door open and let the ten thousand in, hoping that the thousand will unite and save me even though one bite will kill me. Should I just be safe and shut the door? We do have white people saying: 'I mean right, I got a black husband, all my children are black, I love everybody.' I really believe you but I'm sorry, ma'am, there's ten thousand behind you that don't feel that way. What am I going to do? I know. I bet my hand on my family's life that there are some white that mean right but they are so few. I can't forget all the lynchings, the murders because there are two that mean right. When America drops bombs on Vietnam, she drops them on babies and boys. When she dropped the bomb on Japan, they don't say some are innocent. They just at war. When a person in Belfast leaves a bomb, they don't say, well, there's a kid who's innocent in here, there's an old lady who's blind, they just boom, leave the bomb! What I'm saying is, we have a problem and maybe there's a few bosses mean right but there's so many that don't. We have to look at the problem as a whole. I want to make that plain, I know that there are whites that mean right.

There were times in this portion of the interview when Ali appeared to be straining to reconcile Nation of Islam dogma with the reality of his experience in Ireland. After almost a week in what was then one of the whitest countries in the world, a week where his every move had been greeted by uniform adulation and affection, he couldn't just parrot the standard lines about 'white devils' without equivocation. In attempting to adhere to the doctrine of his religion while carefully avoiding causing offence to his hosts though, he was clever enough to get himself out of verbal jams – the question about Angelo Dundee, for instance – by leavening the tension of the moment with wit and humour.

At the remove of nearly thirty years, it is the radicalism of his beliefs that stand out. Anybody too young to have ever seen him fight or to have watched him perform on television in his pomp would find it hard to reconcile this outspoken (if still quite charming) extremist with the sedate figure who has over time become a benevolent, grandfatherly icon in our lives. The thirty-year-old angrily demanding that a separate black nation be established in America was the Muslim charged with the task of explaining to the Western world in September 2001 that his religion was all not about hate.

'Rivers, ponds, lakes and streams – they all have different names,' said Ali on a visit to Ground Zero in New York just ten days after the World Trade Center had been attacked. 'But they all contain water. Just as religions do – they all contain truths. Islam is peace.'

Ali's transformation from the rabid segregationist of 1972 to the ecumenical beacon of 2002 can be traced back to the death of Elijah Muhammad in 1975. Elijah was succeeded by his son, Wallace D. Muhammad, who renamed the Nation of Islam the World Community of Al-Islam, renounced the theory of black superiority and ceased calling for segregation. Ali accepted these new policies wholeheartedly, changed his stances accordingly, and began telling interviewers that 'actions and deeds' mattered far more than somebody's colour. The new direction set him on a journey that brought him to his current status as a UN Messenger for Peace, a man of such standing that in January 2002 he publicly asked the kidnappers of *Wall Street Journal* reporter Daniel Pearl in Pakistan to release him in the name of Allah. What a difference from the man Cathal O'Shannon tussled with all those years ago.

O'SHANNON: You yourself have some little white blood in you.

ALI: Yeah, what are you saying?

O'SHANNON: You feel totally Negro?

ALI: Black? Nobody's really totally, like Chinese are yellow they say but they are not really yellow. You're white but you're not totally white. Gimme something white. (*He picks up a notebook with white pages from O'Shannon's desk.*) See, this is white, you not white, you kinda pinkish. I'm not black but I'm considered black, as far as the blood is concerned. Some people say you talk so bad about us here in America, you got some white blood in you. Oh yeah, how did I get white blood in me? Way back a hundred or something years ago, the old slave master's wife used to get tired and he would sneak back into old granny's shack, and she had big hips, she was pretty, and had big breasts and big legs. She was strong 'cause she worked all day to clean up the white lady's house, raise the white lady's babies and poor white lady was tired and weak, and old black slave lady was strong. He would sneak back at night and close the door and you know what he would do?

O'SHANNON: I can guess.

ALI: You can guess what he would do! And then here come me, half-black! (*He laughs aloud at that as do the crowd.*) They laughing 'cause they know what I'm talking about.

For all the laugher, that exchange was the one where O'Shannon felt uncertain about what would happen next.

'I thought he was going to hit me,' says O'Shannon. 'I'm thinking to myself: "Christ, he's getting angry now!" He clenched his fist and his fists oddly enough weren't that big. He was a huge man, big broad shoulders and a tiny waist, but my Christ, he had a pair of feet on him that were ginormous. He had bloody great boots on these huge feet, yet the hands weren't all that big. But at that point, I began to think maybe I pushed it too far. But then he began to tell me the story of how the slave master snuck around and was full of fun again.'

When O'Shannon brought up the topic of Harold Conrad telling reporters that Ali was a wizard, possessed with magical powers which included the ability to see into the future and put curses on people, he couldn't resist the opportunity to demonstrate his magic. Once O'Shannon had produced some suitable silver paper from his cigarette box, Ali was off and running.

ALI: I can take, for an example to show you my powers, some silver paper and wet it and fold it . . . I can take this right here, for example, and if it don't work, you tell the people the truth, I don't make no promises (*He licks the paper.*) . . . I can take this here and I can fold it up like this. (*He folds it over several times.*) Now, you can give me your hand and I can say just watch me. (*He places it on the back of O'Shannon's right hand.*) . . . And you concentrate, that paper is going to get warm, so warm until it will start smoking until it gets real hot, do you feel it?

O'SHANNON: Do I feel it? (*Uncomfortably shifting in the chair, his voice goes up a few decibles.*) Oh, do I feel it! (*He shakes it off and examines his hand.*) Can I just see it for a second?

ALI: (*Picking the paper off the ground and holding it for inspection.*) Somebody from the audience . . . lady, come here real fast. (*A woman walks nervously on stage holding her handbag.*) . . . Is that hot? (*She just nods her head before walking off again.*)

O'SHANNON: He's a wizard . . . that's not bad. (*The crowd applaud the feat.*)

ALI: The paper is actually red-hot.

O'SHANNON: Quite truthfully the paper is still quite warm, I don't know how that was done but it's not bad.

Shortly after that *coup de théâtre*, disaster struck. One of the recording machines broke down and there was a delay of about twenty minutes. As technicians scrambled to get it running again, O'Shannon quizzed Ali to no great avail about the technique he had used to burn his hand. In the front row, however, Dundee grew increasingly irritated with the stoppage. Like any conscientious trainer, he didn't want an already sick fighter spending too long under the hot studio lights less than forty-eight hours before the first bell. 'Come on, get this thing finished!' he shouted more than once. 'Get it done!' Eventually, the longest wait of O'Shannon's life was over and the cameras were back on.

Beforehand, it had been O'Shannon's intention to get Ali to read something from Jose Torres's celebrated study of him, *Sting Like a Bee*. Dundee scuppered that plan, warning him not to ask his fighter to read live on television. He didn't say exactly why but his tone brooked no argument. Instead, Ali was invited to rattle off one of his poems, and ended the show with the same sort of flourish he finished so many fights.

O'SHANNON: Most of your poems are funny, but you've written one about your own people, I think at the time of the Attica prison riot [On 13 September 1971, a four-day revolt at the Attica Correctional Facility in upstate New York culminated in 1,500 state police and National Guardsmen storming the prison. Of the forty-two people killed in the ensuing violence, ten were hostages taken by the prisoners.] It's a serious poem. You certainly have some very serious moments, as you've shown us tonight. Could you, before you go, say that poem for us?

ALI: This poem explains the Attica prison riot. Did you hear about that over here? All the black prisoners were shot. Just before, they held some white hostages and they said they would cut throats if they didn't get what they wanted. And the word was, well, if the throats were cut, then shoot to kill everybody. They found out during the autopsy that throats were not cut, they just shot them for nothing, the trigger-happy policemen. That [Nelson] Rockefeller [the New York Governor at the time] gave word: 'Ten minutes or so, if they don't give up, open fire.' One black prisoner came out to speak to the warden and the warden said: 'You've ten minutes to surrender or we are going to come in and shoot you, what's your reply? We're going to come in there and shoot!' The black prisoner came out with a poetic poem, this didn't happen but this is what I wrote:

Better far from all I see

To die fighting to be free
What more fitting end could be
Better sure than in some bed
Where in broken health I'm led
Lingering until I'm dead
Better than with prayers and pleas
Or in the clutch of some disease
Wasting slowly by degrees
Better than a heart attack
Or some dose of drug I lack
Let me die by being black
Better far that I should go
Standing here against the foe
Is there sweeter death to know
Better than the bloody stain
On some highway where I'm lain
Torn by flying glass and pain
Better call on death to come
Than to die another dumb
Muted victim in the slum
Better than of this prison rot
If there's any choice I got
Kill me here on this spot
Better far my fight to wage
Now while my blood boils with rage
Less it cool with ancient age
Better valour for us to die
Than to Uncle Tom and try
Making peace just to live a lie
Better now that I say my sooth
I'm going to die demanding truth
While I'm still akin to youth
Better now than later on
Knowing the fear of death is gone
Never mind another dawn.

Then they opened fire on them but they died telling it like it was. (*At the end of a virtuoso performance, he mimics the sound of a machine gun going off. Having listened in perfect silence to his rendition, the audience applauds.*) I've another thing to say, this is one thing, this is one thing I love and admire about the Irish people. I've studied a little history since I've been here, I found out that you been underdogs for years, hundreds of years. People dominating you and ruling you. You can identify with this freedom struggle, you understand, I just have my mind on the other side of the water. But we're all fighting for the same causes and ideas, we just have different reasons and approaches.

8

Ronald Reagan Enters Fat City

I

On Tuesday morning, John Huston's striking silver hair and beard made him stand out among the crowd of two hundred or so shoehorned into the handball alley to witness Ali's last workout before the fight. The photographers present got the Oscar-winning director and the boxer to pose with their fists clenched in classic fight shot mode, and the picture made the front page of Wednesday morning's *Irish Independent*. Huston had also brought a camera of his own and asked Paddy Monaghan to record the image for his own collection. That close to the champ, he didn't want to take any chances with the memory.

An avid Ali fan – he had flown from Spain to New York for the first Frazier fight – Huston boasted a personal history in the sport like few others. At the age of fifteen, he began sparring in a city playground in Los Angeles and carved out a record of twenty-three wins from twenty-five bouts as a six-foot-tall lightweight. Earning $5 a go as a game club fighter, he occasionally fought twice in one night under different names, and for a time, fostered dreams of bulking up to welterweight and snagging a title shot. In the summer of 1923, he accompanied his father Walter to the Polo Grounds in New York where they witnessed Jack Dempsey's dramatic two-round triumph over Luis Firpo.

'Nobody in my lifetime has ever had such glory about him,' said Huston of Dempsey, his first boxing hero. 'He walked in a nimbus.'

Painting and, later, acting lured Huston away from his own

adventures in the ring, but more than half a century after throwing his first punch, he had returned to his first love with a film called *Fat City*. An adaptation of a novel by the poet Leonard Gardner, *Fat City* is a bleak exploration of life in the foothills of professional boxing. Starring Stacy Keach as Billy Tully, a down-on-his-luck alcoholic fighter battling his own demons and the inherent injustices of the sport, it was critically acclaimed when premiered at the 1972 Cannes Film Festival earlier that summer. A week before its New York opening, Huston's press agent Ernie Anderson and Harold Conrad decided that an exclusive screening for the various boxing writers and personalities hanging around Dublin might be a good idea.

Although Huston was then living in Galway, newspaper reports claim that the reel had to be especially flown in from America for the one-off event. While the director and his people were going to those lengths, Ali appeared indifferent to the whole concept. During that lengthy conversation with journalists conducted from his hotel bed the previous day, he had complained repeatedly about how his commitments in RTE had scuppered his plans to go out and see a movie. Even when Anderson reminded him that they had arranged a private viewing of a film yet to be released in America, Ali seemed underwhelmed.

'Huston?' he asked. 'Is he a big movie man?'

Quite a strange question from somebody who was a renowned movie buff to pose. Any time Peter O'Toole wandered into Ali's orbit that week, he referred to him only as 'Lawrence', the role from the David Lean classic with which he associated the actor most. At this point in a career encompassing acting, directing and writing for the big screen, Huston had two Academy Awards and nearly a dozen nominations to his credit. Maybe Ali had never seen his directorial debut, *The Maltese Falcon*, or his 1948 tour de force, *The Treasure of the Sierra Madre*. Perhaps it was that the name in isolation meant less than a face would have. Or it could just have been him acting mischievous in order not to devalue his earlier complaint about having to sacrifice a possible trip to the cinema. In any case, it wasn't long before a reporter mentioned *Man in the Wilderness*, the 1971 film in which Huston played a feature part, jogged the fighter's memory and prompted him to offer a synopsis of the movie. He quickly broadened the theme of the discussion to Hollywood in general.

'I want to make a movie, but the black actors don't play the right parts . . .' he told reporters before starting to hum the theme tune from *Exodus*. ' "Guess who's coming to dinnah? – A black man. Oh, Daddy won't like that but Dora will." '

After a brief pause for breath, he was off on the Hollywood salary scale.

'A guy makes $100,000 in a movie, he's gotta be big in that business,' he said. 'I get $250,000 for one fight. If I make a movie, I want to be like a Charlton Heston. Boum boum. Big blue sky. Boum boum. Desert. Boum boum boum boum boum boum. Then there's that man. Big boum boum . . . The history of King Hannibal. There's a movie for me. They can go back and check his history – he was black. Or let me tell my own life story in movies my own way, just let me do that.'

When Tuesday afternoon rolled around, Ali strolled the short distance from the Gresham Hotel to the Regent Cinema on Abbey Street in his by now customary regal fashion, passers-by stopping to stare at his cavalcade en route. Once inside, he sat in the back row, a few seats behind Al 'Blue' Lewis, and the image of the two relaxing in the same theatre barely twenty-four hours before stepping through the ropes betrays the fight's place in the Ali canon. Notwithstanding the obvious encounters at weigh-ins, it's hard to imagine him willingly sharing the same space as Frazier or Foreman or Liston in a social setting so close to a contest.

A sometimes depressingly realistic portrayal of a type of boxing far removed from the bright lights and glamour of televised bouts and the international media, Ali still found elements of *Fat City* that resonated with him. At one point, a brash schoolkid called Buford, who bears more than a passing resemblance in voice and looks to the younger Clay, tells Ernie

Munger, a rookie fighter played by Jeff Bridges, that he intends to be the 'world's champ' by the time he's eighteen. Sitting in the dressing room before they get called, Buford begins advising the older but less experienced Munger about his bout.

> No way in hell this dude is gonna beat me 'cause he's too old, raves Buford, I'm too fast and I'm gonna be all over him. I'm gonna kick his ass so bad every time he takes a bite of food tomorrow he's gonna think of me.

The eloquence and brio of the young pretender so inspired Ali that he jumped out of his seat, cheering and shouting at this scene: 'Stop the picture, that's me up there, listen to that ... that's me talking! That's me! You hear?'

How he responded when Buford, whose fight isn't shown on-screen, appears minutes later swollen-faced and despondent, reportedly after a dropped left caused him to be knocked out, is not on record. On the way out of the cinema, Angelo Dundee offered the most succinct appraisal of *Fat City*.

'It was good,' he said. 'It was reality.'

Maybe it was too much reality. According to Conrad, Ali didn't find the later stages of the film quite so enthralling as the first half-hour. Indeed, he reckoned that Ali started dozing off at one stage and Lewis was actually asleep towards the end. If Huston was perturbed by this seeming lack of respect for his art, he didn't let on, laughing as the promoter assured him that a movie about the daily grind and sordid underbelly of boxing was probably a little too close to home for a fighter.

Still, when Huston rang Celeste 'Cici' Shane, the woman who later became his fifth wife, in California soon after the screening, it was the moment when Ali stood up and shouted excitedly which he talked about most. As a true fan, the approval, however fleeting of his hero, had meant something.

Like any ambitious young pro should have done, John Conteh went to bed early each night at the Gresham, trying to rest up ahead of his clash with New Yorker Johnny Mack on the undercard. His best efforts at eschewing the party scene building downstairs in the hotel bar were undermined one evening when there was such a sustained burst of activity that he decided it warranted further investigation.

'I remember the police cars and all this bloody noise and lights going off all around the place,' says John Conteh. 'I was seriously preparing for a fight because this was, you know, another step up for me, a chance to build up my record as I went along, and to be fighting on the same bill as Ali meant Americans would see me fight too. So then there's all this bloody noise and lights and it turns out to be Ronnie Reagan. He was lucky he was a senator or whatever he was because I wasn't too pleased with the noise waking me up, I can tell you. I was that annoyed at being disturbed I'd have chinned the guy if I got my hands on him.'

Reagan was in Dublin on the last leg of a European tour, a goodwill trip to seven countries organised on his behalf by President Nixon. The decision to billet the then Governor of California at the Gresham made for some funny juxtapositions. The denizens of the boxing world weren't used to the accoutrements of high-profile American politicians.

'It had been a lousy week weather-wise but then one day the sun suddenly came out,' says George Francis. 'Once I saw the change in the weather, I decided to head up to the roof of the hotel and sunbathe for a couple of hours. I'm lying there catching a few rays when all of a sudden, this swarm of blokes in suits come walking around the roof. They were secret-service types checking that there was no one up on the roof with guns and stuff like that. I suppose it was in case somebody wanted to take Reagan out.'

The security men were certainly taking very few chances.

When Steve Eisner's twelve-year-old daughter Arlynne tried to board the lift to go up to the room she was sharing with her father one afternoon, she found that it had been declared off-limits.

'I was trying to get on this elevator and this big man stood in front of me and told me I couldn't get on because Ronald Reagan was behind him,' says Arlynne Eisner. 'Reagan looked around him and then said: "Ah, let her get on." So Dad and I got on the elevator with him and I was so scared to ask him for his autograph but I did and I got his autograph. He was so nice that he's been my hero all my life just because of that. He said like all of two words to me but was my hero all my life just because of that.'

Don Elbaum, Eisner's colleague in the Lewis camp, had more sway with the Reagan party. Elbaum had brought his girlfriend with him to Dublin. A Vegas showgirl who grew up in a wealthy California family, Diane Lewis knew the Los Angeles and Hollywood social scene intimately. Unbeknown to Elbaum, she made an appointment to visit the Reagans in their suite. When he pleaded a prior commitment at the gym with his fighter, she put her foot down and insisted he accompany her.

'I think Diane's mother was close to the Reagans,' says Elbaum. 'Her family were socialites so she moved easily in those circles. She brought me to the hotel and we were called upstairs and there they were, the Governor of California and his wife. We spent an hour with them, which was dynamite really. Reagan was pretty impressive back then. You gotta remember that normally I would be hanging out with boxing people, a load of half-assed gangsters. This was different and it was great. We had some tea and we chatted. He knew about the fight, he seemed to know a lot about it, actually.'

Unlike his formal visit to Ireland as President of the United States twelve years later, Reagan was far from the centre of attention. The day before the fight, people loitering around O'Connell Street, hopeful of an Ali sighting, were hugely disappointed to discover that the procession of police cars and limos contained a visiting politician whom some of them vaguely remembered as having been a movie star one time.

'The sweating crowd on the steps of the Gresham Hotel at lunch hour yesterday were mostly disappointed when word percolated that Governor Ronald Reagan of California merited the police escort and heavy guard,' wrote Val Dorgan in the *Cork Examiner.* ' "Goddamn it!" an American matron said. "Who the hell said it was Clay anyway?" "Up the Democrats!" I said en route to the foyer. She flashed me a mouthful of perfect enamel and old gold.'

Who the hell said it was Clay anyway? That a member of the Reagan party would still regard Ali as Clay eight years after he formally changed his name is not wholly surprising. The Reagans might have been staying down the corridor from the Conrads but relations between the fighter's camp and the politician's were somewhat strained. This made it all the more interesting when one of the Reagan children took advantage of Ali's proximity to go autograph hunting.

In *The Greatest*, Ali recalls meeting Michael Reagan just after he weighed in for the fight. After a brief conversation during which it emerged that this good-looking, enthusiastic kid was the son of the California governor, Reagan Junior supposedly smiled and made a Black Power salute with his fist. A few minutes later, Ali claimed to have overheard Ronald Reagan himself utter the following to friends as they waited for an elevator: 'I don't know what happened to Michael this morning. Muhammad Ali was down here weighing in and I couldn't keep him in the room.'

While Ali may have been close enough to have eavesdropped, the politician never acknowledged his presence. This was something the boxer felt was inevitable since Reagan had single-handedly prevented him from getting a licence to fight in California during his years in exile. However, we can only take Ali's word for that perceived slight, and that he and his biographer Richard Durham have mixed up the Reagan children hardly bodes well. In July 1972, Michael, Ronald

Reagan's adopted son from his first marriage to Jane Wyman was twenty-seven years old. The boy who approached Ali was fourteen-year-old Ronald Junior.

That said, if Reagan did come that close to Ali by the lifts, the governor could hardly claim not to have known his face and it is undeniable that he had not distinguished himself in his previous dealings with the boxer. Nobody knew more about their intertwined history than Harold Conrad. Before Reagan denounced the prospect of Ali making a comeback in his state, the chairman of the California State Athletic Commission had assured Conrad that his search for a venue was over because Ali finally had enough votes to get a licence.

Conrad's version of events inside the Gresham offers an insight which corroborates the flavour if not the detail of Ali's story. He, at least, gets the name of the Reagan child correct and concurs with the view that Ron Junior was a huge Ali fan, desperate for the opportunity to meet and greet his hero. Conrad maintained later that he arranged for Ron Junior to have his photo taken with Ali and also gave him four tickets for the fight. Most pertinent of all, he wrote in his memoir of a chance meeting with Reagan in the hotel where the governor was effusive in his praise.

'He's marvellous, that Ali,' said Reagan, smiling benignly as he spoke.

Conrad played along with the new spirit of détente but didn't forget that this was the man who had scuppered his plans to promote Ali in California just a couple of years before. In a phrase that became emblematic of Ali's difficulty in finding a place to fight, Reagan reportedly said: 'I don't want that draft dodger ever to fight in my state.'

Eight months after that near collision in the Gresham, Ali finally did get to fight in California, losing a twelve-rounder to Ken Norton in San Diego. Even more shocking for some of his supporters than that defeat was the news a decade or so later that Ali had gone public with his support for the re-election campaign of the then President Ronald Reagan.

III

Once Ali had mentioned to journalists that he was seeing a doctor, the story of his cold quickly became public knowledge. In the bar at the Gresham, the speculation was that the fight might be postponed to allow him to recover from the sickness. This was not an option he ever entertained. When questioned about the severity of his illness by Dave Anderson from the *New York Times* on Tuesday, Ali offered the first glimpse that Dublin was beginning to lose its lustre for him.

'Herbert wanted me to cancel the fight for another week, he's worried about the cold,' said Ali. 'But I don't have a fever and I'd go crazy here for another week. No coloured folks here. Makes me appreciate America. Makes me want to get home. But the cold's in my nose, it ain't in my chest, where it would affect my wind. I ain't seen many black people here, about four. It's like Japan was, I'm an entertainer in these foreign cities.'

Steve Eisner didn't know quite what to make of the 'cold' until Dundee invited him to visit Opperman's the evening before the fight. Upon arriving at the hotel, Eisner sent his daughter out horseback riding with Teri Dundee while he and Luther Burgess sat down to discuss business with Ali's trainer.

'Angelo says to me: "Steve, we've known each other a long time, the champ's got a real bad cold, he's clogged up and I don't know what he's got for this fight, what sort of condition is your kid in?" says Eisner. 'And I was honest with him. I told him "Blue" was about 60 percent fit. He says: "Is that the truth?" Angie,' I said, "I've no reason to lie to you." Really, the fight hung on that whole conversation. If "Blue" was in 100 per cent condition, I don't think they could have taken a chance on going ahead. Not against somebody who could punch too.'

Once Dundee's mind had been put at rest, everybody repaired to the dining room where Ali was holding court in his usual style, eating as much as he wished.

'Ali was sitting at the next table to us,' says Arlynne Eisner. 'And he was eating this huge plate of green peas. And I remember my dad and Luther saying: "He's not supposed to eat peas, it gives him gas. What's he doing? Is he out of his mind? He won't be able to fight properly tomorrow!" We watched him eat for a while and then I told my dad that I wanted his autograph so badly. My dad kept saying: "Go ask him, go ask him." I started getting upset because I couldn't do it. Finally, my dad went up and asked him: "Will you give my daughter an autograph?" "No!" he said. "She has to ask me herself." So I had to walk up and ask him and he gave it to me but I was terrified, I had gotten lots of big stars' autographs but he was different. It was such a big deal that I still have it today.'

When Ali wasn't in the city centre training or promoting the show, there was always something going on in the hotel. Driving up towards the front entrance, a visitor might discover Rock Brynner sitting cross-legged strumming a song on his twelve-string guitar about how Ali would be champ again some day. Inside, Ali could be stalking the floor with a golf club in his hand for the benefit of a photographer, or seeking out new victims for his panoply of magic tricks. John Conteh regularly made the trip out from the city just to hang out with one of his heroes. The two became so close that it was on Ali's advice the following year that the Liverpudlian moved down to light-heavy, the weight at which he became world champion in 1974.

Much like Ali, Conteh still battles the after-effects of life in the ring. During our conversation, he admitted his memory of that week in 1972 was extremely cloudy and he didn't remember some of the anecdotes about Dublin told in his own auto-biography.

Ali's approachability and the widespread knowledge that he could often be found loitering in the lobby at Opperman's seemed to attract every chancer and fly-by-night in Dublin. They came searching for an audience with the champ, fifteen minutes during which they could appraise him of some can't-miss get-rich-quick scheme or other. It wasn't often that a man of such wealth advertised his whereabouts for the duration of his stay in the city and there were plenty of blaggards eager to seize this chance. Most got no further than the dour figure of Herbert Muhammad who reportedly held a suitcase full of unsigned contracts by the time he departed the country. One or two visitors, however, left an indelible impression.

'Butty Sugrue, he was a nice guy,' says Angelo Dundee. 'He was a gentleman and he was a good real-estate man too. He tried to sell Ali one of the islands off Dublin. I don't know which one and I'm not sure he even owned it, but he was convincing Ali all week long that it was worth buying. He kept telling him this little island was a great investment. He was desperately trying to interest Ali in it, and it was a beautiful sight too, but Ali wasn't too accustomed to Ireland, I guess, so he didn't bite. I knew a lot more about Ireland and the Irish than he did. When I was a kid, the Irish and the Italians in Philly always had a certain warmth for each other, so my affiliation with the Irish had always been good.

'It was interesting for us to be there at that particular time though. One of our paper guys, Jack McKinney, was up and down from the North during the build-up to the fight. Jack was deeply involved in the strife and he would come out to the hotel and give us updates on what was going on. My thing about that was how the heck could the Irish not get along with each other? You are a warm bunch of people, how is there so much fighting there? We weren't apprehensive at all about the Troubles, I mean, I had my wife and daughter with me so that shows I wasn't worried and they really fell in love with the place.'

Halfway through Ali's trip, Reuters ran a report on their international news-wire service that his impact on Ireland had been so profound that his presence had moved Ulster off the country's front pages. This was a gross exaggeration. The day Ali arrived in Dublin, a fourteen-year-old Catholic schoolboy was sexually assaulted and murdered by four men with connections to the UDA and UVF in north Belfast. Four others died on the same date and Ali's visit, which coincided with the end of a two-week-long IRA ceasefire, actually came during one of the bloodiest weeks of the entire Northern Ireland conflict.

Thirty-seven people were killed in the space of eight days. Dundee's understandable dismay at the events taking place a hundred miles from where he was staying contrasted hugely with the attitude of Harold Conrad. Where the trainer puzzled over the fighting, the promoter regarded the proximity of such terror as one more convenient selling point.

'And I'll tell you something else,' Conrad told the *Irish Times*. 'It will make a big impact on world news when people look at their papers and see Muhammad Ali walking about Dublin in perfect safety. A lot of people who don't know much about Ireland think you get shot on the streets down here. This will show them that's not the way it is.'

A laudable sentiment somewhat undermined by an incident recorded in his diary later in the week. Walking past Joe Bugner's hotel room, Conrad spotted his manager Andy Smith packing up his bags, getting read to skip town. An unnamed terrorist group from the North had reportedly phoned in a threat to kidnap the English heavyweight and Smith wasn't taking the possibility lightly. Ever the smooth operator, Conrad sat down and talked Smith out of departing by promising increased security for him and his fighter.

'Nobody snatches Bugner,' wrote Conrad in his memoir, *Dear Muffo*. 'I'm disappointed, it would have been a nice touch.'

9

Two Ladies and the Champ

I

In his classic work, *Loser and Still Champion*, Budd Schulberg opens the chapter concerning the first Ali–Frazier bout at Madison Square Garden with quotes from both fighters, from match referee Arthur Mercante, and from the then MP for Mid-Ulster Bernadette Devlin. It says much for the level of international recognition the twenty-four year-old civil rights activist enjoyed in 1971 that among a crowd including Salvador Dali, Elvis Presley, the Beatles and Frank Sinatra, Schulberg felt the sight of Devlin in a ringside seat chanting 'Ali! ... Ali! ... Ali!' was especially noteworthy. Unfortunately for her, not everybody regarded her presence at the sporting event of the year as appropriate behaviour for a serious political campaigner.

'I remember being castigated by the revolutionaries for going to the fight in New York,' says Bernadette McAliskey (née Devlin). 'They felt my presence at the event gave it a credibility it did not deserve. They considered that I should have been on more serious business, and not be participating in these lower-class-type things. I was in the city on political business but Jimmy Breslin, the newspaper columnist who I happened to know, he had got two tickets for myself and the woman I was travelling with. We weren't going to pass them up, two tickets, good seats in the house to watch Ali fight. Of course, we got hammered by the political activists for choosing to be there as opposed to being at some serious political work.

'That experience got my head around the whole notion that thou shalt not laugh until the revolution is over! But it was fascinating to be at Madison Square Garden, just to experience the whole aura of the place. It was amazing to see these two poor craturs, two black people fighting even while people around the ring, racists in that place still managed to be racist, hated them for the colour of their skin. Their anger, their prejudice was so totally against Ali. Those things stuck out for me. That fight was heartbreaking. I just kept hoping he'd pull it out. You knew he wouldn't but still, you kept hoping. It was a dynamite night.'

Not quite twelve months later, Devlin was on a makeshift stage, atop the back of a lorry, addressing civil rights protesters in the Bogside in Derry when British paratroopers opened fire. Within seconds, she found herself under the truck fearing for her life. Within eighteen minutes, thirteen unarmed civilians were dead and another sustained wounds that would later cost him his life. That date, 30 January 1972, would go down in Irish history as the second Bloody Sunday. The following day, Devlin was in the House of Commons to hear Home Secretary Reggie Maudling, the minister with responsibility for Ulster Affairs, announce the establishment of a government inquiry into the event. When Maudling baldly stated that the troops 'returned the fire directed at them with aimed shots and inflicted a number of casualties on those who were attacking them with firearms and with bombs', Devlin leaped to her feet on a point of order. After the Speaker of the House dismissed her objection, she shouted: 'Is it in order for the minister to lie to the House?' Maudling endeavoured to continue as uproar ensued on both sides of the chamber. Devlin denounced him as 'that murdering hypocrite' before marching to the centre of the floor.

'I screamed at Maudling,' said Devlin in a 1972 interview with *Playboy*. 'I grabbed him by the hair with my left hand and punched him in the face over and over again with my right. Ted Heath, brave man that he is, was right next to him, terrified, white as a sheet. He started crawling up the bench away from us. Maudling just stood there, stunned, while I punched him, his fat mouth hanging open in shock. And then the chief whip, Francis Pym, staggered over and gallantly tried to protect Mr Maudling. He was too much of a gentleman to hit me so he just got tangled up between us. His breath alone was strong enough to win the battle. Suddenly, the whole thing was so farcical that my anger just drained away. Bob Melish, the Labour whip, intervened at that point. He was trying to look outraged but couldn't stop laughing. "Bernadette," he said, "that's quite enough." I'm proud to say that was the first time in history a lady ever assaulted a Cabinet minister during a session of Parliament.'

Even after being escorted out the door, Devlin returned minutes later to defend her assault, shouting: 'I did not shoot him in the back, which is what they did to our people!'

Little wonder then that a few months down the road, somebody in the Ali camp decided she was the type of person Ali might like to meet. The parallels between their lives are quite striking. Ali stood up to the US government on the issue of the draft, Devlin stood up to the British government in the battle for equality for all in Ulster. He was the youngest heavyweight champ, she was the youngest woman MP. He styled himself as the poor black boy from Louisville. In her maiden speech to the House of Commons on the day of her twenty-second birthday, she declared her presence to be 'the arrival of a peasant in the halls of the great'. He came mighty close to going to prison for his beliefs and actually did ten days in a Florida penitentiary in 1968 for driving without a valid licence. She served four months in Armagh jail in 1970 for her involvement in the Battle of the Bogside. When invited to visit Ali's camp on the day of the fight, she didn't think twice.

'My main recollection is of being totally overawed at being there in his company,' says McAliskey. 'He was just a lovely man, really sharp, really bright and witty. A very equitable sort of man. You know there was none of this "I'm the champ" about him on a face-to-face level. It's kind of hard to explain. He had a lot of charisma. Here we were, we were all just down from the North and we were fairly ordinary people, and whatever bit of name recognition I had, it would have meant nothing to him. As far as he was concerned, we were all just ordinary punters, yet we were treated just magnificently.

'People say to me you know you must remember things like hitting Reggie Maudling and I have to scratch my head but Ali I remember vividly. It was, at the time, the whole excitement, the aura of it, and people at home not believing you had tickets for it, never mind that you had sat down and eaten dinner with Ali in Dublin. I used to find that hilarious. None of the other famous people I met impressed my constituents at all but they were all nearly shaking my hand after that – not because I had gone through hell for them – but because mine was the hand that had shaken the hand of Muhammad Ali. I just remember it was a wonderful cameo of excitement that had nothing to do with events up here.'

Her travelling companions that Wednesday morning were Michael McAliskey, the man she would later marry, and his friend Frank Gervin, both of whom were deeply involved in amateur boxing with the Coalisland and Clonoe clubs in Tyrone.

'I've no recollection of any in-depth conversation about the North. He knew who I was but that wouldn't have been too hard at that time. I suppose that would have been pointed out to him. But he was equally friendly and interested in the people who were with me, who were running small, rural boxing clubs in the North. He was just a genuinely interesting person, not one of the people who behaved like a celebrity. There was no showmanship about him in private, just a lovely man, very intelligent actually and a good conversationalist. He was such good company.'

Bernadette grew up the second eldest in a family of six in Cookstown, County Tyrone. Her father died when she was nine years old and given that her only brother was the youngest child, she still struggles to comprehend how the house came to be dominated by two sports and two particular names: Manchester United and Muhammad Ali. When she sat down for lunch with Ali that day in Dublin, she found herself breaking bread with a man she had idolised since childhood. Even for somebody who had attained such a degree of fame that, depending on which side of the political fence you were on, she was either 'a miniskirted Castro' or an 'Irish Joan of Arc', gaining an audience with Ali was intimidating.

'I was surely nervous on the way there. I don't have many heroes, I don't go in for heroes, but he was a hero. I was totally overawed. I was nervous because I was out of my area of expertise and out of my depth. But then to find that sitting down for dinner with him was like sitting down with your mates, to be welcomed into the circle the way we were, that nervousness dissipated quickly. I do remember that a part of me was really saying: "Oh God!" beforehand. I think part of me was concerned about what it would be like if the positions were reversed. Here was I going down to meet a hero of mine but he was probably saying: "Why do I have to meet these people?" I mean, I wasn't in line with the Taoiseach or even the head of Macra Na Feirme at that stage, I was more like the local troublemaker not yet disposed of.

'I'd have been in his corner all my life. He was very important to everyone in that sense, not just important to young black people. He took principled and difficult stands. When you look at him today I think he still does. We don't want that image of power and prowess we associate with to dissipate. His willingness to be in the public arena in his present health condition does away with a lot of the myths that in order to be in the public eye, you must stay at the top, at the pinnacle. Here is a man famous for his speed and skill now struggling to maintain balance, to find words and to stop his hands from shaking. Others in his position might say: "Oh, no one should see me like this." Well, it's equally courageous and radical to be out there now in his physical condition.'

It was quite a day for Devlin. That morning, the Irish newspapers had all put a story about Reggie Maudling on their front page. After allegations were made about his involvement in a financial and political scandal known as the Poulson Affair, Maudling had handed Prime Minister Heath his resignation as Home Secretary. Taking her seat in Croke Park – a venue she had previously visited for Gaelic football matches – after hours spent in Ali's inner sanctum, Devlin couldn't help comparing the atmosphere in the ground to that which she had experienced in Madison Square Garden just over a year earlier. Then, she was shocked at the abuse being showered upon Ali from all levels of that arena. Now, the volume of support and the affection being displayed towards him made the contrast all the more striking.

'Croke Park was so different when I remember the abuse he took in Madison Square Garden. I think that Ali was not aware until he came here about the overwhelming support for him in Ireland. And that would have been understandable. Imagine coming here from America; as far as he was concerned, he was coming to Europe and everybody here was white. He would have not understood that we only look that way, that we're not really white at all. As pale as the driven snow we might have been, but the warmth of the welcome and the identification people had with him didn't fit with the colour relationship. That was an eye-opener for him as well; I know it was not something he expected in Ireland.'

Ali was equally taken with Devlin. In conversation with Paddy Monaghan, he described her as 'one of the world's great ladies'.

Hearing the compliment relayed after nearly thirty years, Devlin laughs at the language used by Ali.

'One of the world's ladies? Lady had a different connotation in his circle than it did in ours. I think he used it in that old-fashioned way, whereas we would use woman. The way the Protestant community would use lady in that sense, they would consider it rude to speak of a woman as a woman. They would say "A lady called." And we would say: "Had she a Lord with her?" I think it must be something to do with the Baptists.'

II

Elgy Gillespie lives in San Francisco now, working as a food writer, and has a scar on her left hand, the story behind which must sound to so many people in her present life like a tall tale. Two pale dots, each the size of an aspirin on her skin bear silent witness to the time she once spent in the company of Muhammad Ali and his extended family. As a twenty-two-year-old cub reporter, she sat in Opperman's one afternoon, took Ali up on an offer to demonstrate his awesome powers of concentration, and became the unwitting dupe in yet another rendition of his favourite magic trick. A familiar old routine, it found new victims everywhere he went. Witness Cathal O'Shannon taking the same bait.

Asking Gillespie to focus hard on her packet of Carroll's cigarettes, he then requested that she tear off the foil from the top. When she did this, Ali licked both sides of the foil, folded it into a small, neat square and placed it on top of her hand.

'Now stare deep into my eyes,' he said.

She obeyed the instruction and soon felt the first inkling of a burning sensation on her skin. Ignoring the discomfort, she continued to play the part until her hand began to smoke alarmingly. Only the intervention of an extremely annoyed Odessa Clay broke the spell of concentration. When she removed the foil, Elgy discovered two blisters. A delighted Ali held up his hand and waved it in front of her eyes. It was then she spotted the residue of white powder on his fingers. She returned to the *Irish Times'* offices in D'Olier Street that night but none of her colleagues could figure out exactly what substance would react with tinfoil and spit to form an acid.

'People always ask me: "What the hell did you let him do that for?" It's not a badge of honour, it's a badge of shame in some ways. What was I thinking of, letting this guy burn my hand? It was interesting that he decided to try to do it at all and what was more interesting is that his mother interceded so suddenly, saying: "Stop it Cassius!" She called him Cassius, and he looked kind of confused. To her, he was still Cassius, and to him, he was probably still Cassius a little bit too. I suppose it was more original than an autograph, at any rate.'

Barely a year out of university, Gillespie was assigned the job of interviewing Muhammad Ali. As a task, it was equal parts invigorating and nerve-racking. None of her superiors told her how best she might wangle a personal audience, and not knowing where to start looking, she turned to Sammy McDonald, a business journalist and a friend from their days together in Trinity College, for advice. It was his idea that Gillespie should get up early in the morning, go to Opperman's and try to catch Ali doing his roadwork.

'I was quite dubious, I thought, well, he'll hardly want to talk to me, he's the most famous man on earth, how the hell am I going to get near him? Sammy said: "Why don't you get up early in the morning and go running with him?" "I can't do that," I said. "Firstly, he won't let me, and secondly, I can't get up early in the morning anyway." I was living above a pub at the time and somehow by staying up all night, I managed to get my arse over to the hotel in south Dublin the first day and I just hung out there. Sammy had told me to stay there and stay there and stay there until people start talking to you, and if you don't get to talk to Ali himself, you'll get to talk to his people, and that's what happened.' Just by being around the lobby, Gillespie fell into the company of Odessa Clay and gained the sort of access that turned her full-page story, published in the *Irish Times* on the morning of the fight, into that week's best piece of journalism, by some distance.

'Mrs Odessa Clay sits in a spankingly new beige leather chair, looking out of the window, bored,' wrote Gillespie. 'She is everybody's idea of the motherly mother, except that she is far more beautiful than most mothers. She has a pale complexion and a broad serene face with delicate features; she seems to spread a little lake of calm about her. She spends a lot of her time waiting, waiting; although she travels all over Europe with Ali, one would guess that she never saw much farther than a similar hotel: a glass tomb with a view. I ask what they think of the hotel: they think it's real homey . . .

'Ireland seems pretty cold to her after Kentucky, and yet she's heard that the temperature never goes below fifty degrees in winter. Is this really true, she asks. "It's because of the sea," I start to explain. "Can you tell me what sea we are in? The Atlantic?" Mrs Clay is very surprised at how peaceful the streets of Dublin seem to be: can I explain a little of what's going on here? I take a big breath: "Well, it's a bit like this, see, in the North, there's more Protestants than Catholics so, you might understand it easier this way, you might say the Catholics were a bit like the blacks in America; they don't get the best jobs, see. But down here, it's all different because there's more Catholics than Protestants because mostly they've left, but it's not the other way around quite . . . do you get me?" '

Gillespie got to observe Mrs Clay doing the little things that mothers do. When somebody bounded into the lobby one morning and announced that Ali was still asleep, she wondered aloud if she should take her son his shaving kit or leave him at peace. Few thirty-year-old men are as mothered as that.

'I ended up taking Odessa around Dublin. Odessa was a very beautiful woman. She was a bit confused, however, she kept looking at the sea and asking: "Is that the Atlantic or the Pacific?" Mrs Clay was one of nature's fools and so am I, so I think we had an immediate understanding of each other. I was a bit stunned that she didn't know where she was and I felt protective of her. She was puzzled and she gave me the impression she was worried about her son. She was worried about him in a sort of "what has that fool boy got himself into now?" kind of way. She loved him dearly and felt a great need to protect him, but I got the impression that thought had passed through her head a lot since he was born. We discussed her Irishness. There's an awful lot of Irish blood in black Americans and inevitably they have a certain ambivalence about it because very often it comes from somebody taking advantage of somebody. In fact, though, they are not ashamed of it.'

Her budding friendship with Odessa Clay yielded an introduction to her other son Rahaman. Of all the members of the entourage who had embraced the Muslim faith, Rahaman Ali struck Gillespie as the most devout student of Islam. 'May you receive all the wonderful blessings of goodness that life has to offer you,' he wrote in a note to the journalist before delivering her a stern lecture on the evils of smoking. Eventually, Rahaman arranged a private audience for Gillespie with his brother, albeit one framed by certain bizarre conditions.

'It was Angelo Dundee and Rahaman who told me not to use a tape recorder or to take notes. I spent a long time listening to Ali and because of this restriction I ended up running around the corner intermittently to write stuff up and down my arms and legs. I didn't tell him I was doing it and I felt bad about that. I felt like I had broken some rule, but really I had no choice. When I came back to the office after that interview, I was literally hitching up my clothes to read his quotes. I had an innocence about me then, I didn't know what I couldn't do. I had lots of fears and anxieties but I had the fearlessness of the completely ignorant and dumb, if you know what I mean.'

Her shorthand must have been flawless because every quote in Gillespie's piece certainly sounds like the authentic voice of Ali. Some might argue it was unethical to take notes in so clandestine a fashion, more would wonder why any restriction was placed during an interview with the twentieth century's most loquacious sportsman in the first place. Whatever the merits of those arguments, the quotes are vintage Ali.

On the subject of power: 'I have no power. What power have I got? I've a heavy cold which I can't seem to get rid of. Who made the sun that warmed me as I ran this morning? Who made the milk I drank last night? Who made the steak I ate? Who made the grass to grow so as the cows could eat it? Not me, I couldn't make it. I ain't got no power. When I'm the biggest man in the world I could be struck down by a germ or I could be crippled by disease. And I know that. I know that I'm nothing, same as everyone else.'

On wealth and opulence: 'I got cars and a house, sure, but I only got one suit. When people see me they say: "Why aren't you driving around in a white suit in a limousine with two girls on either arm? Why are you dressed modest?" And back in my home in the USA, the newspapers, they write about me as though I was public enemy number one. Muhammad Ali, enemy of the people. But I don't mess with a limousine and all that. My place is on the sidewalks and in the ghetto, sitting back on the garbage cans with the drunks. That's where I am. Because I want to be bigger than anyone but I want to stay big and strong with my own. I want to be on top of the great big mountain but at the same time, not selling my soul, not selling out as they say.'

On Ireland and the Irish: 'I like it fine here because I know real sincerity when I see it.'

On his future: 'Well, if I went lecturing now, most people wouldn't be interested. There wouldn't be no more than a few. But if I got James Brown and the Famous Flames and the Temptations and Ray Charles and the Jackson Five along in the hall, people would come. But if it was just me, I'd have to make music – doo-dah doo-doo – to bring folks to me. So what I'm doing is I'm trying to make it so big that everyone comes to hear me lecture.'

On violence: 'When I was called up, I thought I can't go and shoot those poor people I ain't never seen. I can't do that. In the old days, I fought wild, I landed a punch, wham, and I said: "I got you!" And I go [rains down blows on an imaginary foe]. I was mean. But now I don't want to hurt the man. You seen me in the Quarry fight? I asked the referee to stop it, I held off. Now I make the big hit, I see I've got him and I hold off so as not to hurt him.'

On his troubles with the draft: 'That was no suffering. The trial and that, that wasn't no suffering. I enjoyed that. That was a challenge. That made me bigger than five Joe Fraziers could ever be. What was I doing? I was taking on blond, blue-eyed America, and the power elite, the power structure. It wasn't suffering, but if my mother died . . . well . . .'

On the insatiable public appetite for autographs: 'I think about it like this. I get a little fellow coming up to me, asking for my name. He's little and to him I'm big, real big. And when he's got my name, he's real proud and happy and he runs off shouting.

And to me, it's just a little thing, no more than a couple of seconds.'

As a student journalist in the late sixties, Gillespie was fascinated by all forms of radicalism. She'd spent a summer working in Cuba, and another in America where she had read closely about the Nation of Islam, and it was this aspect of Ali's character and belief system rather than the fighting that intrigued her most before she arrived in Opperman's that first day. The overview she gained of Ali's religion was not as edifying as she had imagined. At one point, she ended up ordering gammon steak in the hotel restaurant just because it was prohibited by the Nation of Islam.

'Rahaman was very strict about his beliefs and he talked to me for a long time about religion. I think he was under the impression that he was making great headway converting me to Islam because I was just drinking it all in and listening. Some of the other members of the Nation of Islam were strict in one way and then, they were ludicrously licentious in other ways. I felt it hadn't dawned on them that you can't be a strict Muslim and retain an entourage of five prostitutes. They hadn't really gotten the concept clearly.'

During her conversation with Ali, the talk turned to women, white women in particular. An unnamed member of his party had arrived back at the hotel the previous night with two women on each arm, much to the boxer's disapproval.

'Man, he had four blondes on his arm,' said Ali. 'I don't hold with that. You see these big black fighters, they go for white women. You see Diana Ross, she married a white man. And a whole lot of others, any blacks make it big, I mean really big, they've always tried to make it with whites. They're not really big. I want to be bigger than any of them and stay with my own people.'

At this juncture, Ali's friend, the man last seen ferrying four women to his room arrived into the lobby, looking slightly bashful.

'I saw you, man, I saw you last night,' chided Ali, his stern tone betrayed by his facial expressions. Out of the corner of his eye, shielded by his towel, he half winked at his pal, who sat off to the side, trying to ascertain if he had grievously offended Ali's moral sensibility or not.

Of course, the manner in which Ali's own prolific love life – Dr Ferdie Pacheco described him once as a 'pelvic missionary' – contradicted his religion so blatantly that it must have been difficult for his friends to decipher whether their promiscuity offended him or not. Indeed, when Gillespie asked him about fighters worrying about forthcoming contests, he turned his answer into a meditation on infidelity.

'Man, I never worry. More people die from worrying than almost anything else,' he said. 'You get the young boy, he's done something wrong and his mother says to him: "You wait 'til your father gets home, he's going to see you." So he waits all evening, waits six hours, and all the time, he's worrying. And he's saying to himself: "I'm so scared, what's my father going to do to me when he comes home?" And that's the worst part, because when the father comes home, wham-bam it's all over.

'Or you get the man, he's got a girl and he gets this girl pregnant and he's married. For nine whole months, he's worrying about what he's going to do, how he's going to see her in the hospital and how he's going to look after her. When all he's gotta do is go to his wife and say: "Look, wife, I was out late last week and I was weak . . . what are we gonna do about it?" That's all. No, I don't worry . . . not a lot. I think. I think all the time about this world and the people in it.'

It wasn't common knowledge at the time but this last quote held particular relevance for Ali's own personal life that summer. Patricia Harvell, a girlfriend of his in New Jersey, had recently given birth to a daughter whom she named Miya Ali. Whatever way Belinda reacted to this obvious confirmation of his heavily rumoured dalliances outside their marriage, the couple didn't actually divorce until five years later.

Elgy Gillespie kept a promise she had made to Rahaman Ali and posted him off a copy of her article for his files. Months later, he wrote back and told her he had found the piece hugely entertaining but couldn't believe his brother had said all those things because nobody had seen her take a single note during the conversation. It was, she supposes, a kind of compliment.

10

Gloves Are All You Need

ALI TO WIN SOON AFTER SIXTH – *Irish Independent*, 19 July

BUTTERFLY ALI TO FLOAT HOME BUT AL STINGS LIKE A
  BEE! – *Irish Press*, 19 July

ALI EXPECTED TO DISPLAY HIS MASTERY – *Irish Times*,
  19 July

From the exploits of Peter Corcoran and Duggan Fearns in one
century through the bare-knuckle antics of John Morrissey and
John L. Sullivan in another, the story of boxing is intertwined
with the path of Irish history. So many of the first great batch of
fighters were either born in Ireland – Yankee Sullivan came into
the world in Bandon, County Cork – or to Irish families abroad
– 'Gentleman' Jim Corbett's parents had made it all the way to
San Francisco – that it's no surprise the country became
synonymous with the sport.

   If Harold Conrad and Butty Sugrue were hoping to tap into
this tradition by staging a contest in Dublin, they obviously
didn't realise that despite the rich heritage, the capital city had
never been a hotbed for professional boxing. Quality bouts had
been few and far between. World heavyweight champion
Tommy Burns dismissed Wexford's Jem Roche just under
ninety seconds into the first round of their farcical title clash at
the Theatre Royal in 1908, and most of the spectators complained loudly that the Canadian hadn't even given them time
to place their top hats beneath their seats. Croke Park itself was
the venue when Bartley Madden and Tom Heeney, a pair of
heavyweight contenders, did mediocre battle in 1925, but the
previews of Ali–Lewis all alluded to a more storied encounter
held two years prior to that fight.

On 17 March 1923, Mike McTigue wrested the world light-heavyweight crown away from 'Battling Siki' before a crowd of 1,500 at La Scala Theatre on Prince's Street. Born in Clare but boxing out of New York, McTigue took a controversial decision after twenty rounds against Siki, the enigmatic Senegalese, also known as Louis Phal, whose decision to fight an Irishman in Dublin on St Patrick's Day meant his only real hope of victory was a knockout. This point was emphasised just before Siki entered the ring when the theatre shook violently, the city centre having been rocked by an explosion that reminded everybody involved that outside on the streets the civil war still raged.

For bringing the big-time fight game back to town after such a lengthy hiatus, Messrs Conrad and Sugrue caught a lucky break with the weather. The hottest July day since 1955 offered them hope that those without tickets bought might yet be encouraged to make their way to Croke Park. After all, what better way to spend the twilight of a day where the newspapers predicted a high temperature of eighty degrees than watching Ali fight? Buoyed by the climatic conditions, Conrad was in fine form strolling through the lobby of the Gresham, awaiting the arrival of the fighters for the eleven o'clock weigh-in. Spotting Raymond Smith in a throng of reporters around Billy Conn, he took no prisoners.

'Hey, you, Smith, you'll get your press ticket for the fight all right,' shouted Conrad. 'We never lock out the media but the crows will have a goddamn better view than you'll have.'

Conrad remembered Smith from the previous April as one of those who were scoffing at the very thought of Ali coming to Dublin to fight. With just hours to go before the first bell, he was entitled to his fun. In any case, Smith found out soon enough that he had actually been given a ringside seat. Perhaps his nemesis had been too distracted by subsequent events to exact revenge because no sooner had the weigh-in passed off without incident in the hotel ballroom – Ali at 217 lb 8 oz, Lewis at 223 – than the true extent of the disorganisation came to light.

The souvenir programme to be sold that night didn't contain a single article, just photographs of Ali, Bugner, Henry Cooper, Jack Bodell and Danny McAlinden, the last three heavyweights, of course, having nothing to do with the promotion. Lewis didn't merit a single head shot, and the main event was listed as a scheduled ten-rounder. Worse was to come, and soon the tawdriness of the programme was the least of everyone's worries.

'We had lunch and then a small meeting inside the Gresham,' says Barney Eastwood. 'Everyone was saying: "That's it now, everything's finalised." So as we were walking out, I said to somebody: "Now, who has the gloves?" Somebody else says: "Yeah, who has the gloves? Who has them? We need gloves for the fighters." After much searching and panicking, it emerged that there were no gloves of suitable quality to be had in Dublin. It must have been nearly three thirty in the afternoon and the first fight was due in at six thirty. I rang a pal of mine in London, a jockey called Gary Hart and I told him to go round to the British Boxing Board of Control, and see if he could get six or seven sets of gloves, tie a string around them and take a taxi straight out to the airport. In the meantime, I'd see if I could get him on a flight. There was nothing more we could do at that stage.

'Despite our best efforts, the fighters still ended up sitting in the dressing rooms with no gloves on as we waited on news of Gary. Now, remember, in those days there were no mobiles. Eventually, my man appeared with all the gloves tied up with the string, he'd done everything to get to Croke Park from London on time and this was about twenty to seven, the boys were in the dressing rooms and the first fight was being called and there were no gloves. My mate Gary was outside and, despite the fact that half of Dublin was getting in free, they wouldn't let him past the gate. When he went around to the main gate, and said: "My name is Gary Hart, I've come here from London with the gloves for the fight," the security man said: "You'll have to try a better story than that, I'm not letting you in." Finally, somebody sent word or somebody saw him, he got in eventually, and the first fight went off around seven.'

At roughly the same time as the evening's entertainment had begun in Croke Park, there were some bizarre scenes back at the Gresham. When somebody sent out word that Ali was in the building awaiting his transport to the venue, an estimated crowd of more than a thousand filled the lobby and the steps outside. Among them were two skinheads who had earlier been asked to leave the premises after management discovered them blocking the entrance to the lounge. Upon returning and attempting to gain re-entry, the skinheads asked the security guards on duty to bring Ali out because they wanted to fight him.

'One of the men returned later and demanded he had the right as an Irish citizen to be let into the hotel,' went a report in the *Irish Independent*. 'A scuffle broke out and he was hauled into a Garda patrol car. His clothes were torn from his back as Gardai and security men tackled him. As the crowd grew, Special Branch men and Gardai surrounded the building. Traffic was at a standstill and guests had to be escorted into the hotel. The entrance was sealed by a protective gate as the security force was stepped up. Many visitors sat in the hotel porch to view the scene.'

Up in Croke Park, the action had already begun. A week in the company of Ali put John Conteh in fine form to open the bill against thirty-three-year-old Johnny Mack, a journeyman whose flabby midriff and losing record betrayed his standing in the sport. Unfortunately, Conteh was to find his path to victory interrupted before it began. Just because there were now real gloves available in the stadium didn't mean the logistical problems were over.

All psyched up to go to war, Conteh lost some momentum when an official insisted on personally trying to put a left hand glove on the Liverpudlian's right fist. Although George Francis saw the humour in the moment, his fighter did not. When the matter was finally resolved the only person bound to suffer the butt of Conteh's anger was his opponent.

From the bell, Mack made no attempt at combat, retreating into defensive pose for the duration of the first round. Half a minute into the second, Conteh caught him with a right cross and a left hook that merited a standing count. Less than sixty seconds later, the referee stepped in to spare the hapless Mack further punishment.

'The same official who gave John the two left gloves ended up giving me a pair of six-ounce gloves for him,' says George Francis. 'Those were gloves for a little flyweight. John would usually have needed at least an eight-ounce glove. But John had slim hands and we wedged the gloves on and when he hit Johnny Mack on the chin, it was a case of "Good night, nurse!" We weren't going to argue about the gloves. I'd heard strange things happened in Ireland; my attitude has always been to go along with the place you're in, when in Rome do like the Romans do.'

Around ringside, the best seats in the stadium were being taken by the most famous names. Jack Lynch took time out from the crucial Mid-Cork by-election to fulfil his promise to Ali. Eamon Casey, the then Bishop of Kerry, was sitting next to the Taoiseach, providing a buffer between him and Neil Blaney, whom Lynch had sacked as Minister for Agriculture two years earlier during the arms crisis. Bernadette Devlin was only one of the politicians from Ulster present. Paddy Devlin, chief whip of the SDLP, sat in Croke Park oblivious to the fact his home had come under fire during a gun battle involving the British Army on Shaw's Road in Andersonstown that evening. One shot went through the window of his sixteen-year-old daughter Moira's bedroom.

'I was doing the ironing when these shots were fired and took the three children up to the upstairs landing,' Mrs Devlin told the *Irish Press*. 'The shooting was fierce. It's not a nice thing to say, being an MP's wife, but I feel like running away from here.'

After Conteh's curt dismissal of Johnny Mack, there was the much anticipated appearance of Joe Bugner. His opponent Paul Nielsen was a twenty-two-year-old Canadian who flew to Dublin as a late replacement for the American heavyweight

Charlie Jordan. When fifty of his compatriots contributed $50 per person so he could turn pro, Nielsen had earned the nickname 'The Investment'. That he was willing to come to Ireland at such short notice to fight Bugner was indicative of how badly he was struggling to make good on that moniker.

'When John's fight was over we went and sat on the grass to watch Bugner,' says George Francis. 'The nice thing for me was that I'd trained a lot of Irish kids over the years in St Pancras' in Camden Town and there were guys coming up to me in the field saying: "Hello, George, remember me, you used to train me." That was all very pleasant, and though Bugner's wasn't a good fight, it was fun to watch because Mickey Duff was constantly shouting: "Stop it, ref, stop it, ref." When that didn't work for him, he went over to the corner where Joe was and started shouting: "Come on, Joe, you've got to do better than that." All Mickey wanted was the fight to be over and Bugner to look good. Anyway, he's running around the ring the whole time and we're all laughing. We could see exactly what he was trying to do. Poor old Mickey.'

Bugner made heavy work of defeating Nielsen in what was arguably the worst contest of the evening. Seemingly bent on staying in the ring for as long as possible, the Canadian was repeatedly warned for holding his opponent. Fifteen seconds from the end of the sixth, the ref decided he'd do what Bugner couldn't and finish the thing.

'One of my main memories of the night was that Joe Bugner couldn't box,' says Bernadette McAlisky. 'Man, I couldn't believe him that night. I had no idea until I saw him what an absolute sham Joe Bugner was. It's terrible to say that it overshadowed the night for me but he was so bad. He didn't look like a boxer, he didn't box like a boxer, and he got away with it. From beginning to end, he was a sham. That stark contrast with Ali, this incredibly multi-talented and intelligent, fine figure of a human being who was being picked on around the whole world and only begrudgingly accepted for being as good as he was. And then you had this other geezer who was in total contrast, this great big slobber who had difficulty making any impression and this myth surrounding him, this myth that he was something when all he was really was white. He had nothing else going for him but that was some advantage.'

From late afternoon, there had been people milling around the Jones Road entrance to Croke Park in anticipation of Ali's arrival. Without wanting to buy a ticket for the fight, they were hoping to see the headline act on his way into the stadium. He gave them all the slip when gaining entry at the other side, although, optimists that they were, many of them stayed waiting in that location until well after his bout had actually begun. Once inside his dressing room, Ali stretched out for a massage from Luis Sarria. As the Cuban worked his magic, Ali was coughing and sneezing repeatedly.

Any pre-fight tension was dissipated by the arrival in the inner sanctum of the television personality, Eamonn Andrews. As previously arranged with Ali, Andrews approached the fighter's second and announced 'Paddy Monaghan, this is your life!' Thrilled by the shock registering on his friend's face, Ali asked: 'What you gonna do now Paddy? You on *This is Your Life!*' Before Monaghan could even react, Ali's smile gave the game away. Paddy never did get to tell his life story to Eamonn.

When Andrews left, Dr Ferdie Pacheco injected cortisone and Xylacene in between the webbing of the fingers on both of Ali's hands. Since the comeback, Pacheco had been doing this to numb the fists and allow him to punch at full force without feeling the pain. While all this was going on, Pat McCormack was sitting in an annexe outside the room, preparing himself ahead of his bout with France's welterweight champion David Pesenti. Son of the legendary Spike, McCormack had his older brother John with him to work his corner that night. Their first-hand experience of Ali suggests he was in pretty relaxed form before the fight.

'We didn't even know Ali was in there at first,' says John McCormack. 'But there were a couple of policemen posted outside the dressing room and I kept saying to Pat: "I wonder what those policemen are doing standing there, Jesus, they must be expecting trouble." So Pat says to me, messing: "That bleeding bum is in there, Muhammad Ali." "Jesus," said I, "do you think he'll come out?" So anyway, after a while, Angelo Dundee comes out and we ask him whether Ali was inside. When he said that he was, we told him we'd love to meet him. Angelo goes back in and Ali came out then to shake hands with us.

'That was my first time seeing him up close and I said to Pat: "I don't know whether to shake hands with him or kiss him, he's bleeding gorgeous." Ali looks at me and says: "Are you a faggot?" I thought he was calling me a maggot because I'd never really heard the word faggot before then. "What kind of talk is that," said I, "calling me a maggot." "I said faggot," says Ali. Anyway, Angelo Dundee butts in then and says: "Tell him your name." When I told him McCormack, Ali says: "Are you a Pole?" Whatever way the name sounded to him, he thought I was Polish. "No I'm not, I'm Irish, I'm from Dublin here." "Oh!" says Ali, "lovely to meet you." '

Pat McCormack put Pesenti on the canvas twice before the referee stopped it in the Dubliner's favour at the end of the fifth. Quite an achievement considering the curse of the dreaded gloves appeared to have struck again, and for a time McCormack looked like he'd be fighting with one hand bare.

'Pat had only one glove on him when he got in the ring as a matter of fact,' says John McCormack. 'There was murder over that later. It could only happen in Ireland. The way a night of boxing goes, they like to get fellas in straight after each other to keep the momentum going. The fella they called the glove steward wouldn't give us the gloves for whatever reason and I was trying to say to him: "You'll have to give us the gloves early because people are trying to get into this tunnel to see Muhammad Ali come out in the minute and if we don't get out there before they all file into the tunnel, we won't be out there at all. There'll be no fight for my brother."'

Back in his dressing room, Ali had joined Rahaman and

Herbert Muhammad in a pre-fight prayer to Allah when a knock on the door was followed by a voice saying: 'Whenever you're ready, Muhammad.' What he encountered upon walking through the door must have been quite a surprise.

'I saw Muhammad Ali coming out of the dressing rooms,' said Paddy Maguire, a Belfast bantamweight who had just decisioned another Frenchman, Guy Caudron, at the end of an eight-rounder that was the best contest of the evening. 'I don't know why but there was this wee Corkman standing there, and he was telling people where to go. The set-up was that you got your bandages wrapped in the dressing rooms, then you went to get them signed and approved, and finally, you put your gloves on when you got in the ring. This wee Corkman says to Ali: "You've to go and get the bandages on your hands stamped by the officials." Muhammad didn't understand him because the wee Corkman had an accent that made him sound like he was singing when he was talking. Muhammad just stops and starts to dance around him and says: "What do you say, Dad? What was that, Dad?" And he just keeps on at him like that, you know the way Ali carried on. The poor Corkman didn't know what to say and then Ali just danced away.'

Paddy Byrne was Maguire's trainer that night.

'This very old boy was in charge outside the dressing rooms,' says Byrne. 'When Ali arrived, this old boy, who looked the spit of Barry Fitzgerald and must have been about eighty, says: "Don't you put your gloves on until the Irish Board are present." Ali thought he was joking so he shaped up to this old boy as if to fight him. But this old boy was very serious and we had to try to cool him down. It was unbelievable. I thought to myself, this old boy wants to fight Muhammad Ali. He was dead serious, he'd lost his rag with Ali. He was looking to fight him and Angelo Dundee was looking at me as if to say: "You're Irish, you do something about this."'

Those already in their seats had been kept entertained by master of ceremonies Michael O'Hehir. The legendary commentator conducted an auction to raise funds for the mentally handicapped, the highlight of which was Pat Quinn forking over £1,000 for a painting of Arkle. O'Hehir also adhered to the usual big-fight ritual of bringing every celebrated boxer in the stadium up on to the stage for an ovation. The spectators cheered local heroes, Freddie Gilroy (a bantamweight from Belfast who won a bronze medal at the Melbourne Olympics) and Martin Thornton (a heavyweight known in his 1940s prime as 'The Connemara Crusher'), just as heartily as Jose Torres, Billy Conn and the former world middleweight champion, Terry Downes.

'I just came over with a few guys,' says Downes. 'We felt Ali was as near to us in London as he might get for a long time so we just went over for a couple of days to see the fight. We had a hard couple of days drinking but you didn't have to be that sober to take in the fight. I'd seen him fight in London, spent time with him when he was training in White City and that, so I didn't go to watch him sparring in Dublin, I just turned up for the fight. Just wanted to see the great man again.'

Apart from eyeballing the famous names in the crowd, the spectators were amused by lots of unplanned slapstick taking place around the fights. O'Hehir nearly had his head taken off by a swing stool as he climbed into the ring to announce one of the fights. A poorly constructed press bench collapsed with one end of a timber plank bloodying the face of a journalist. More than one of the undercard bouts contained rounds that lasted nearly four minutes instead of three due to poor time keeping at ring-side. And every joker in Dublin decided that standing up and encouraging each fighter by shouting 'Go on, hit him, you have the wind behind you' was hilarious. It might have been the first ten times somebody said it. As the countdown to Ali's arrival drew near, Rock Brynner strolled into view, carrying a camera and wearing an outfit that drew a collective gasp from onlookers who must have thought him one more act in the sideshow.

'Brynner's son was walking around taking photographs,' says John McCormack. 'We'd never seen anything like him before, this guy in a big white kaftan with a broad-brimmed hat. The whole place was staring at him and a fella shouted: "Who's that there, he's like something from the Ku Klux Klan?" Then word went around that it was actually Yul Brynner's son.'

Brynner took a seat directly behind the Taoiseach, largely oblivious to the impact he'd had.

'It was such a lovely evening for a fight,' says Brynner. 'There was a gorgeous sunset, the stars were starting to come out against the blue sky and I saw flocks of geese flying overhead.'

After avoiding further entanglements with officialdom, Ali made his long walk to the ring. Apart from Dundee, Pacheco, Sarria and Monaghan, Sugrue had augmented the security presence around his headline act with the Brereton brothers. Having built the ring twice, the men from Edenberry were given the honour of delivering Ali to it.

'All I could hear as we walked along was the crowd shouting: "Go on, Muhammad! Up ya boy, Muhammad!"' says Joe Brereton: 'They were going on like that the whole way in. We brought him to the corner and then we had to find seats near as we could to the corner. I ended up next to the film star Peter O'Toole. He had a bottle of gin, and believe it or believe it not, I drank half it with him. He was a decent man, he passed it over to me every time he took it out of his coat. I wouldn't normally drink gin neat, but sure when you're getting it for nothing, why wouldn't you?'

Wearing a white robe with his name emblazoned across the shoulders, Ali climbed into the ring and the crowd erupted. Just three months before, the prospect of the former heavyweight champion fighting in a stadium on the northside of Dublin would have been dismissed as the stuff of fantasy. Now, everybody felt they were on first-name terms with him. 'Up ya boy, Muhammad!' They had seen that face so often on their black-and-white televisions, poured over newspaper and magazine articles about his various antics, but this of course was different. Yards from their seats, he strode towards his appointed corner with a determined look on his face, his eyes purposefully avoiding Al 'Blue' Lewis's best attempts to stare him down. This was for real. No matter that he was being paid handsomely for his trouble, he had come to their town to put on a show, and as the appointed chorus, they too had a role to play in the evening's performance. They cheered his every move during the pre-fight formalities, each nuance a novelty worthy of their applause. When he leaned repeatedly against the ropes to test their elasticity, even that warranted a prolonged ovation from the adoring hordes. It was as if they interpreted that manoeuvre as a sign he meant business. Around Ali, Angelo Dundee, Ferdie Pacheco and Luis Sarria fussed, like they had done before so many other fights past. Paddy Monaghan chewed a matchstick between his teeth and intermittently fingered the inside pocket of his jacket where he had safeguarded his prized second's licence. And outside the ring, the crowd waiting for the first bell to toll, and for Dublin to earn its place in the Ali chronicles.

The Mountain comes to Muhammad

The night before the fight, Harold Conrad was drinking in a pub off O'Connell Street when he got into conversation with a local man, who informed him he was going to the fight.

'Have you bought a ticket?' asked Conrad.

'I'm going but I ain't paying,' answered the Dubliner. 'It's an affront to ask an Irishman to pay to see a fight.'

'Did someone give you a ticket?'

'Nobody gave me a ticket, but I'll be there.'

'How are you going to get in?'

'That's for me to know and you to find out.'

Conrad could get nothing more out of him but an enigmatic smile that stuck in his mind the next night when he looked around the stadium. The upper decks of the Hogan and Cusack stands were empty, the terraces at each end equally so, and, despite the clement weather and Ali's masterful salesmanship, it looked like they would struggle to reach the break-even attendance of 30,000.

Later, some people would blame the fact that Al 'Blue' Lewis just wasn't glamorous enough to sell tickets. Whether that contributed to the financial problems or not, Lewis entered the ring, eager to give value for money. Wearing a black robe that billowed in the slight evening breeze, he bounced up and down on his toes, shadow-boxed and generally gave off the air of a focused sportsman. With scarcely any promotional commitments – there was just one photo op involving diminutive comedienne Maureen Potter standing on a chair next to Lewis after he took in her show *Gaels of Laughter* at the Gaiety Theatre the previous Friday night – he'd been able to concentrate on his training. There were times in the recent past when he'd struggled to find the motivation to train, but notwithstanding one particular instance of trouble in the camp, his preparations for this bout had gone especially well.

'Chuck Nary was a loudmouth guy who hated blacks,' says Don Elbaum. 'But he'd given Al some money and owned a piece of his contract and had this attitude that kept reminding Al that he worked for him now. Al got so upset with him that he refused to go to the gym one day just to show Chuck who was boss. Then I got so mad with Al. I went into his hotel room and said: "Al, you're not going to fuck yourself and you're not going to fuck me. Screw this other guy, you're going to train every day." Then he and I got into this argument, and I said: "Al, if I have to, I'm going to come up here with a baseball bat and you are going to the gym, and if you even think of going out at night, I'll stand by the door and smash your head in." Al started laughing because really, he could have picked me up and thrown me through the window if he wanted to.'

For years, Lewis and his handlers had tried in vain to get their man in against the biggest names. Now, he stood moments away from his date with the biggest of them all, a point reinforced for him by the knowledge that the kitchen appliance company Moulinex were paying £2,000 for the privilege of advertising their name on the shirts of his cornermen. On the canvas in the middle of the ring was a red box containing two sets of eight-ounce boxing gloves. To accentuate the drama, and no doubt fool the public into believing the whole operation had run very professionally, the Irish Boxing Board of Control had sealed the box before it was delivered centre stage. Counting the denizens of both corners, there were so many people (a headcount of the video footage revealed twenty at one stage) overseeing the preliminaries that the ring looked more like the scene after rather than before a fight.

The numbers had been swollen by the arrival of the Dubliners. The Irish folk super group clambered through the ropes carrying banjos, guitars and fiddles to prepare for their rendition of 'Amhran Na bhFiann', the Irish national anthem.

Jumping the gun, the man in charge of the public address system seemed to misread their arrival as a signal and, without any fanfare, the first notes of a threadbare version of 'The Star-Spangled Banner' came crackling through the loudspeakers. The song had barely begun when the pause button was pressed and Michael O'Hehir stepped up to the mike. 'Ladies and gentlemen, the American national anthem.' The tape restarted and this time around everybody did their best to observe the formality and stand to attention. Moments later, O'Hehir tried to put manners on the chaos again. 'And now,' said O'Hehir, 'Ladies and Gentleman, the Dubliners and the Artane Boys' Band will combine for our own national anthem.'

The fight was being broadcast on closed-circuit television in the US as a joint venture by Bob Arum's Top Rank Inc and a company called Video Techniques in New York. Arum was at ringside working as co-commentator alongside Reg Gutteridge. Watching the Dubliners launch into 'Amhran Na bhFiann' and the crowd taking up the singing with them, Gutteridge told his international audience: 'Well, this is a very cute way of playing it.'

Everybody in the ring was standing with their backs to Hill 16, the most storeyed terrace in the stadium. Before the musical interlude began, it was one more barren space. However, the playing of the Irish anthem appeared to be the signal for a mass influx of non-paying customers through the tunnels on the Hill. They were throwing themselves over the fences, sneaking through gates, doing what they had to do to get in.

'They didn't get the crowd they expected,' says Elbaum. 'When we stood up for our national anthem, I looked around and said to myself: "This is an awesome venue for a fight, it would look great with thirty or forty thousand but they could have held this fight in a hall, we didn't need no stadium." Then they played the Irish anthem and everybody was standing to attention and halfway through that song, I swear to you, it was like the scene in a western movie when the Indians appear over the horizon. Thousands of Irishmen came in over the walls and fences and nobody made a move to stop them. It seemed to happen on cue; sing the Irish anthem and everyone gets in free. Wherever the holes were, they found them, so the place filled up a bit. It seemed as though far more people came in free than paid.'

An announcement came over the tannoy: 'Security and stewards to Hill 16, please.' Maybe the sound quality wasn't great because apart from two uniformed Gardai who strolled towards the terrace before turning around halfway, the response of the organisers was non-existent. 'Will people kindly go back to their seats?' went another desperate request. Later, Conrad would estimate that 7,000 got in free.

'All the fellas sitting up in the gods started to make their way towards the pitch then,' says John McCormack. 'There was a wire fence around the field to stop people getting in who hadn't paid for the ringside seats, but sure fellas just came down and started climbing over the fence. They were making announcements over the loudspeakers asking the stewards to go all over the place to stop people climbing over the gates. But they weren't going to stop the Dubs, the Dubs were bunking in and that was it. They didn't care who was there. You had all these young fellas in jeans sitting there with fellas in suits who'd forked out serious cash to be ringside.'

The best seats in the house cost £15 while the most distant standing spot on the terrace went for £2. There were also decent locations available for £10 and £5. Not that the price scale mattered too much to those who had gained access through Hill 16.

'A couple of my friends were working as stewards for the night,' says Mick Daly, who watched the drama unfold from a seat in the Hogan stand. 'Once the fight was about to start, they took seats in the centre of the pitch. They heard the call go out for stewards to make themselves known and eject the Dubs who were getting into the expensive seats, but my friends were sensible enough: they discarded their stewards' badges and stayed in their seats to wait for the fight to start.'

Meanwhile, O'Hehir ploughed on with the introductions and Lew Eskin, editor of *Boxing Illustrated* magazine, referee and sole judge of the contest made his first appearance. Summing up the informed views on what might transpire, Gutteridge mentioned to his audience that Eskin sometimes moonlighted as a firefighter and this could come in handy if Lewis ended up being seriously hurt. Delivering his instructions to both fighters in the centre of the ring, Eskin wiped excess grease from Lewis's forehead. Then Ali returned to his corner, bowed his head and adopted the familiar pose for one more moment of prayer to Allah.

The first round was predictably tentative; the only highlight came when Ali, responding to the exhortations of Dundee who shouted 'Hook him, hook him' all through, connected with a powerful left hook that stunned Lewis. Towards the end of the round, he offered a few left jabs of his own by way of a response, but neither fighter seemed especially enthusiastic for the fray in those opening exchanges. Just before a barely audible bell sounded, a voice from the crowd urged: 'Come on, Muhammad, send him back to the penitentiary.' Despite the lackadaisical pace, Lewis was puffing hard on the way back to his corner and a cut inside his mouth was already leaking blood.

'Al could fight inside and that was the plan,' says Elbaum. 'That was our shot, with the idea that he might tire him out in the later rounds. The other thing was Al could punch, I don't care what kind of a chin you got, if you hit the guy right you can put him in trouble, and put him on the floor. I had told Al: "You go the distance with this guy and we're sitting pretty from here on in. We can make some serious dough." So we had him trying to get to the body early, but unfortunately, nobody could take body shots like Ali.'

During the interval, the crowd were invigorated by the appearance of a short-skirted round-card girl. Betty McDermott, who worked in a local hotel, made a lap of the ring to resounding catcalls and cheers. The timekeeper must have been one of those most taken by her because nearly a minute and a half elapsed before he rung the bell for the start of round two.

Another staid three minutes ensued. Ali was warned for punching low by Eskin; Lewis brushed him back with a decent left hook and almost scored big with another right. Still, when Ali backed him into a corner at one stage, he curiously allowed him out again without landing a solitary punch. Recognising perhaps that he was feeling the ill-effects of his cold, Luther Burgess was manically shouting at Lewis: 'Fire, fire, let punches go.' His charge didn't respond and it was Ali who finished the stronger, unleashing a combination just before the bell.

The third round promised more entertainment. Ali began by dancing around the ring and the crowd rose to their feet to applaud. This was the fighter they had come to see. Lewis was rooted to a spot in the centre of the ring as Ali shuffled around him, clockwise, then anticlockwise, picking him off as he went. But again, Ali ran out of steam and slowed down the pace until he found himself in a corner taking some good body shots. They looked better than they were, because after Lewis had let fly, Ali waved his right hand, inviting him back to deliver a few more. In true pantomime style, Lewis waved his left at Ali in copycat fashion. That this was the extent of the drama sums up a round that ended with Ali shoving Lewis around in his corner.

'It looks like Ali wanted to pin him in his corner then to save himself the walk back,' says Reg Gutteridge, commentating. 'But Lewis is certainly doing a better job than Jerry Quarry did.'

As had become the pattern, Ali was on his feet awaiting the start of hostilities long before the bell for the fourth, and he produced some more shuffling that appeased the small band of spectators who could be heard slow handclapping the lack of real action. The two men traded flurries when Lewis caught Ali in a corner, but it was the Detroit boxer who suffered most when a right visibly weakened his legs. The slight buckle in his knees prompted a shout from Dundee: 'He's tired, he's tired. Use the hook.' Belying the obvious signs of fatigue, Lewis actually ended the round in good fettle, landing a few body shots, the effects of which were negated by the way Ali had his arms tucked by his sides in defence.

'The promoters had put a wrestling mat on the floor of the ring instead of a boxing mat,' says Pete Hamill, then a journalist with the *Village Voice*. 'And as a result, Ali couldn't get up on his toes and dance as he liked to do. A wrestling mat being thicker, there is much less bounce than in a boxing mat. From that point of view, he showed me for the first time that night that he could fight inside, stand there flat-footed and really fight inside. It made for an interesting fight because it showed me he could mix it as a fighter without resorting to the classic Ali style.'

At a press conference the previous day, Raymond Smith had mentioned to Ali that his editor wanted an estimate of when the fight might end, in order to plan the different editions of the *Irish Independent.*

'You go and tell your boss that I will knock the bum out in the fifth,' said Ali. 'Because he can only bring in enough money in advertising on television for that many rounds, I won't carry him any longer than that.' For good measure, he then demonstrated the sort of punch that would end the contest.

Without quite replicating the exact punch, he did all he could to make good on the prediction. Having spent much of the fifth seemingly content to work his opponent's body, Ali had been winded by a right cross that was really the only major Lewis offensive in the round. With thirty seconds to go, Lewis extricated himself from a corner and appeared out of danger. He was right in the centre of the ring when Ali measured him up with a left and dropped him with a right.

'I was pretty short so I had to stand up on my chair to see over the edge of the ring,' says Arlynne Eisner. 'I'd been pretty bummed out that everyone was cheering against Al because I'd grown up around him. When Ali knocked Al down then, my dad could see I was upset. So he leaned over and shouted to me: "Don't worry, he's just put his legs up and that's a signal, he's getting back up, that's our code. Don't worry, he's going to be OK." And he did, he got back up from that one.'

His recovery was assisted by a long count from Eskin that drew criticism from Ali's camp.

'The count lasted twenty-two to twenty-three seconds,' claimed Angelo Dundee's brother Chris afterwards. 'It would have been all over then if the count had been right.'

The fight would certainly have ended there without complaint. Many spectators got up to leave as Lewis hit the floor and even Ali raised his arms tentatively in triumph. But Dundee's timing was off. Lewis was down for exactly fifteen seconds, long enough to lose the fight, short enough for Eskin to offer some respite.

'There was nothing wrong with the count at the end of the round,' said Eskin later. 'Some folk in Muhammad Ali's camp have been saying that it lasted more then twenty seconds instead of less then ten seconds but that is wrong. I did not begin to count until Ali moved away to a neutral corner. Not more than three seconds could have been lost between the time Lewis went to the canvas and Ali moved back to a corner.'

The bell gave Lewis an immediate chance to catch his breath and rehabilitate further. He looked in poor shape, though, as Ali scored with left after left in the opening minute of the sixth. As soon as Ali began to employ his right too, it appeared only a matter of time before Lewis went down for good. More than once, the aftershocks of a punch travelled all the way to his knees, yet each time he stayed upright. Eventually, the bandages on Ali's right hand glove came loose and he eased off the pressure. Buoyed by this latest reprieve, Lewis summoned new reserves of strength, producing excellent combinations the delivery of which was abetted by Ali taking a breather on the ropes for the last thirty seconds of the round.

'I thought that it was a helluva performance by Ali, a man who should have been in bed fighting the flu,' says Barney Eastwood. 'He should have been in bed two or three days before the fight and I really thought for a time it wouldn't even go ahead. Watching him then fight the way he did, I said to myself: "That's a great, great fighter there, you need a special quality of a man to go out and do that under those circumstances." I think his people didn't want him to fight but he wanted to go in, get on with it and get out, and he probably thought Lewis was a soft enough thing anyway. As it turned out, Ali was carrying a big handicap into that ring and Lewis must have realised the other guy wasn't half his usual self.'

The seventh was similar in style and content to the previous round. In between long periods of inertia, Ali punished Lewis whenever he caught him on the ropes or in a corner without ever exerting himself unduly. Then, as the clock ticked down, Lewis emerged from his hibernation to try and do something before the bell. With Ali significantly ahead on points, the storyline had become less about Lewis's chance of effecting a shock and more about his bravery in the face of a far superior fighter. Before the start of the eighth, Conrad made a circuit of the ring, stopped by the commentators' seats and whispered to Arum: 'He just won't fall! He just won't fall!'

For the majority of the eighth, the most animated individual on view was Angelo Dundee. Conscious of the fact that no matter how tired or how far behind he was, a puncher like Lewis could produce something dangerous, Dundee kept on urging his man to 'finish it, finish it'. It was all in vain because Ali gave his left most of the round off and delivered nothing but rights for over a minute. The cumulative effect of that relentless assault can be gauged by the fact Lewis didn't even have the energy for his by now customary end-of-round flurry.

'There's nothing I admire more in a fighter than courage and this guy Lewis certainly has that,' says Gutteridge, as the bell sounded for the start of the ninth.

The leisurely pace of the eighth must have worked wonders for the stamina of both fighters because the ninth was action-packed. A round that began to the soundtrack of more slow handclapping from a belligerent pocket of the Hogan Stand exploded into life. Ali upped the tempo and launched an all-out attack, spending thirty seconds working Lewis to the head and body without having to take a single jab in reply. The crowd were enthused by this but there was never any indication that Lewis was going down under this barrage. Even when battered against the ropes, his legs appeared steadier than before. Then he shocked everybody by going on the counter explosively. Using the ropes almost as a springboard, he went right back at Ali. After succeeding with three stinging rights to the head, the crowd raucously voiced their approval of his efforts. If staying in there with Ali was a genuine achievement, offering such robust resistance with almost nine rounds in the books was worthy of their highest praise. In his corner, they watched his revitalisation and for a moment, just one fleeting moment, fostered real hope that he could yet do something extraordinary.

'"Blue" hit Ali with one really terrific punch,' says Steve Eisner. 'And he armbarred him and I was screaming: "'Blue', hit him with one more, for Chrissakes, one more." And "Blue" looked back at us and shouted: "I ain't got one more. I ain't got one more." Luther says to me: "Shit, we got to put more brandy in the water." If you look at the tapes of the fight, Luther and I put brandy in his water to help "Blue" and he doesn't spit it out after the third round. We had him swallowing it from then on just to try to get him through.'

Ali exacted quick revenge for the embarrassing cameo he'd endured at the end of the ninth. He opened the tenth with a couple of swift lefts to the head and soon Lewis's right eye was nearly swollen shut. Sensing his opponent had nothing left, Ali picked him off at will, wobbling his legs more than once as Lewis, his mouth agape, desperate for oxygen, struggled to land a solitary punch in reply. It had become only a matter of time.

In Ali's corner, however, there was some concern. When he sat on the stool, he emitted a loud groan that worried his trainer.

'Did he catch you in the balls?' said Dundee.

'No, no, my nuts are OK but, oh gee, I sure am bursting.'

Now that Ali had finally subdued Lewis, nature was calling.

'What's the next round?' asked Ali.

'It's the eleventh,' said Dundee.

'I'm gonna have to open up on him in this round because I'm just bursting.'

At the start of the eleventh, Lewis lingered just a few

moments longer on his stool, the body language of a beaten fighter. In contrast, Ali was already up and waiting, anxious to make good on his promise. He danced around his shattered opponent, scoring as he pleased, and Lewis, his hands down by his sides, managed just two feeble jabs in the course of a minute and fifteen seconds before Eskin stepped in. The concerned way the referee embraced him suggested he knew better than anybody that this fighter had earned every penny of his purse the hard way. Ali raised his hands in the familiar pose of triumph, the crowd roared its approval and in a fitting end to the proceedings, Lewis walked across to Ali's corner and lifted him in the air to the delight of the fans.

'The end came, not for any one blow, but from the effects of a great accumulation and variety of shots,' wrote Val Dorgan in the *Cork Examiner*. 'Lewis, a pathetic, groping figure, reeled away with his hands up to his eyes. The referee intervened and in a sport which often suffers from a lack of sportsmanship, the end was expected. The former bad guy, Lewis, gathered his remaining strength to rush to Clay's corner and lift him in the air in a sign of submission which was not lost on the crowd.'

It was about then that the real fun started. Within thirty seconds of Eskin stepping in, the ring had filled up with bodies. Some were television people there for a reason, others were just people chancing their arms. With nobody there to stop them, dozens of fans seized a unique opportunity to get close to their idol. As the crowd around Ali's corner grew out of control, the only person battling to keep the ring clear was Harold Conrad. Waving what looked like a rolled-up poster, he personally shoved and manhandled several interlopers back out through the ropes. His efforts took on a comic appearance in the face of the relentless tide. No sooner did he send one fan on his way than a ten-year-old came sidling through the ropes, shadow-boxed his way across the apron for the benefit of the cameras and was then subsumed by the throng.

Conrad was genuinely shocked by the mayhem that ensued. The sight of so many previously well-behaved patrons clambering over press benches and barging through the ringside where the Taoiseach, Jack Lynch, was sitting became one of his most enduring memories of the whole evening. Having grown up in Brooklyn, where the Irish cop was a uniquely respected figure, radiating authority and never ever suffering fools, he couldn't understand how badly prepared the Gardai were for the onslaught of punters who thought nothing of shoving a uniformed cop out of their way. While most of the action was around Ali's corner, over on the other side of the ring Lewis and his camp were battling against the increasing bedlam too.

'As I'm towelling "Blue" off, this Irish guy is climbing up the ladder and is trying to muscle me out of the way,' says Eisner. 'I turn to him and say: "Will you let me towel the fighter off, please? Give me a moment, I'm working with my fighter." He mumbles something back at me – it could have been in Gaelic because I didn't understand it in all the noise. I turned around and said: "Fuckit." I hit him with a hell of a right hand and he landed right at the feet of an Irish cop who looked up at me. I'm thinking that I might as well put the manacles on because I'm going to the big house. Suddenly, the cop looks up at me and yells: "That was a fine punch!"'

An announcement came over the tannoy requesting more Gardai and stewards to the ring area, but reaching the centre of the crowd became an impossible task. Nobody could get in or out as every passageway was blocked by people. In the ensuing crush, four children were injured.

'We couldn't believe they rushed the ring,' says Angelo Dundee. 'I suppose it was better that they wanted to see him rather than not wanting to see him. In the midst of it all, Muhammad turned to me and said: "Hey, there sure is a lot of nice people here, they all want to shake my hand." We didn't mind that too much and he certainly didn't, he enjoyed that kind of stuff. Ireland gave a different feeling to other places we'd been, we encountered a legitimate warmth everywhere we went in Ireland and that was just one more manifestation of it.'

In the photographs of the incident, Ali looks, at various times, bemused, irritated and downright angry. The home-town press didn't spare the rod when assessing the tumult they had witnessed.

'The ringside was busier than Grand Central Station in its heyday, and when the big fight ended, it would have been safer in Vietnam,' wrote Sean Diffley in the *Irish Press*. 'They rushed in from all quarters, treading the seats into splinters and one woman used my shoulders and then my head on her hopeful way to join Muhammad and all the rest in the hectic mayhem inside the ring. What she and the rest hoped to do there was not clear – the mass hysterical stampede would be a more fitting field of study for a psychologist! Overall, this notable occasion, the appearance of one of the greatest athletes of our generation, was tarnished by the bad manners of the Irish public.'

Even after a semblance of order was restored and enough uniformed Gardai were on hand to begin escorting Ali out of the ring, the crowd were reluctant to let him go.

'People who had been generally well behaved just wouldn't let him get through to the dressing rooms,' says Peter Byrne, who covered the fight for the *Irish Times*. 'He was going nowhere, until suddenly this little Dublin guy who was ready to take the moral high ground jumps up on the apron of the ring and addresses the multitude. "The champion has given us a great night's entertainment," he says. "Now be fair, Muhammad wants to go to his dressing room." A pregnant pause for a few seconds and then this voice comes back: "Let the dressing room come to Muhammad, we're not moving!"'

Twenty-five minutes after Eskin had called a halt to the contest, Ali finally made it to the sanctuary of his dressing room. Outside the drama continued to play out.

'It was charmingly Irish, an Englishman said, as he picked himself up off the ground,' wrote Nell McCafferty in the *Irish Times*. 'We got caught up in a jam in the pitch-dark alley under the stand. Peter O'Toole managed to get his friends through and a tall Negro said to a policeman: "Whaddya mean am I in Clay's team! Look at my face, will ya?" He lit a match and the crowd opened before him. A very nice police inspector took me through, all the way into the dressing room, where Angelo Dundee became apoplectic. "He's naked, he's naked, we can't have a lady in here." His loins were in fact covered with a towel, but modesty dictated that I leave at once. Would that the same decorum have applied to the ring where a young lady in short skirt and white knickers climbed through the ropes between rounds to display a placard announcing the number of each round.'

After Ali had finally relieved himself in the toilet, he lay down on a couch and asked to be given a few moments respite before meeting reporters. Suitably rested, he was effusive in his praise of Lewis.

'I was never worried at any stage but this was much tougher than the Quarry fight,' said Ali. 'I am delighted that we now have shown how good Lewis is. That guy has some real guts, man, and I am not sure if the public here realise just how tough and how strong he is. I hit him with some of my best shots at different stages of the fight and still, he just stood there. There were times when I could not believe it. I would rate him number five in the world. I had a cold and apart from that affecting my breathing, I think I have been boxing too much and am getting stale. He hit me with a few tough ones. Cold or no cold, a couple of times, he hit me very hard and I'm glad I proved that he is worthy of a crack at the best.'

There were close to fifty journalists crowded in there and when one of them mentioned the presence of the Taoiseach, Ali slipped smoothly from gracious victor to gentle braggart.

'If I had known Mr Lynch was here, I would have finished the contest in the third round,' said Ali. 'I am very honoured indeed to have the head of the government come along to enjoy seeing me win. I have fallen in love with this country and the first real break I get from the boxing game, I intend to accept the invitation of Mr Terry Rogers of the Boxing Commission to bring my family over to Galway in the west of Ireland for a holiday. After Patterson, I hope Joe Frazier will fight me and then I will relax in Galway.'

Down the corridor, Lewis was trying to turn a gallant performance into his calling card for future business.

'I want to meet Ali again back at home in the States,' said Lewis. 'I know I can beat him after I've got a few more fights under my belt. When I went into the ring tonight, it was the first fight I had in eight months. I know I hurt him and I also know that I have the punch to floor him. I am also prepared to come back to Ireland for a fight with the Irishman Dan McAlinden.'

As is always the case, the loser's dressing room was a more spacious venue.

'I thought Lewis was an extraordinary character so I decided to focus on him afterwards,' says John O'Shea of the *Evening Press*. 'At one stage, I was the only journalist in his dressing room after the fight and I witnessed this scene involving Lewis and this kid. I don't know what the relationship between Al and this kid were. All I recall is Al "Blue" Lewis trying desperately to explain to this kid that it wasn't the end of the world that he lost. The child couldn't understand what he was trying to say and it was a very pathetic sight.'

It wasn't the end of the world for Lewis, but as the estimated attendance figures were becoming available, the scenario was looking apocalyptic for some.

'We did not lose any money,' said Sugrue when asked about the official attendance of 18,725. 'However, there simply was no profit and unfortunately we have nothing left over for the charity. This fight did put Ireland on the boxing map of the world and we now have the experience to run further shows here. I was disappointed at the response of the leading Irish firms. Perhaps they will offer more sponsorship if we put on another show.'

In truth, no area of the promotion had been left untouched by chaos and bad management.

'This will tell you about the kind of conmen that were around that night,' says Joe Brereton. 'A nephew of mine was selling programmes and this fella came up to him with a badge, pretending to be a steward, and asked him for his money. I don't know where he got the badge but he got away with a handy sum of money off poor Seamus. I don't think he was the only young fella to be ripped off by this guy either that night.'

Those used to filling Croke Park to the rafters for hurling and football matches had their own idea about what went wrong.

'I would hope that the promoters might have a better understanding of the kind of money Irish people are prepared to pay for a sporting fixture,' said Sean O'Siochain, general secretary of the GAA. 'If the Cusack Stand had been priced at £2, I think they would have filled it and made more money.'

An argument for another day. That night, everybody who'd read the papers during the build-up knew that a crowd of under 20,000 meant the promotion had been an unmitigated financial disaster. The best Sugrue could offer the press was a hope that more countries would buy the tape of the fight and alleviate the losses. His partner wasn't even bothering to think that way.

'While the final figures are not yet available, I'm afraid that we are going to incur a substantial loss on the undertaking,' said Conrad. 'The weather was perfect, the best boxer in the world was on the bill, yet the crowds did not attend. It was an artistic success but at this stage I'm not interested in any further promotions in Ireland. If we couldn't make money with this show, what chance would there be?'

Unperturbed by the failure to bring the people in, Conrad did what Conrad liked to do best that night. He and Mara Lynn hosted an elaborate shindig in their suite in the Gresham that went on until early morning.

At one point, he found himself deep in conversation with a Dubliner who congratulated him on the promotion of the fight. This particular patron praised the manner in which Conrad had got the combatants to appear authentic and enthusiastic in the ring when the bout was so obviously staged. For the New Yorker who had seen and heard everything, this was another first.

Conrad's festivities were ending round about the time Ali's entourage were checking into Dublin airport on Thursday morning. An early flight to London would allow them to catch a connection to the States and journey back to normality. Ali never has made that return trip to Ireland. But aside from the tape of the fight itself, he bequeathed the country another unique memento of his visit. For Bord Failte, the Irish Tourism Board, he recorded a promotional video that was shown to American audiences before the fight. Over a montage of quintessentially Irish images like whiskey-making, fly-fishing and thatched cottages, Ali delivered the following script.

'Here I am in Ireland where every visitor gets a thousand welcomes,' said Ali. 'They even gave me the Irish shillelagh to help me win my fight but I don't need it. They told me this was the Emerald Isle. Believe me, they're right. I've never seen such a green country in all my life, not even Kentucky. The Irish people, I have found, are very proud of their ancient history and culture, just like I am, and they preserve a lot of their old customs. They have kept up ancient skills here that have disappeared in most nations and countries. One thing especially about the Irish people that they kept boasting to me about was how good they are at making whiskey, of all things.

'They say that their whiskey takes a long, long time to make but the funny thing is it don't take long to drink. Whiskey is such a big thing here in Ireland that they even go as far as to call it the water of life. And that's crazy. Ireland is also famous for its horses and the Irish people are crazy about all kinds of sports. That's why I'm the greatest also here in Ireland. They even have their own special games called Irish football and Irish hurling. They look pretty rough to me, these football and hurling players, I think I'll stick to boxing. I've been training for my fight so I didn't get to see all of the beautiful country of Ireland this time, but I promise you, as soon as I destroy ugly Joe Frazier, I'm coming back to Ireland with my family and I'm going to have a real rest and a true holiday.'

Tangled up in Blue

Ali's early departure had caught many reporters off guard and the farewell of Al 'Blue' Lewis wasn't exactly a media event. But the ever-resourceful Raymond Smith made his way to Dublin airport to see off the beaten fighter and his entourage. With seven bottles of Guinness safely packed in his luggage for the folks back home in Detroit, Lewis was all set to go.

'I asked him where he had lodged his purse and he indicated a concealed pocket at his waist that I now noticed was distinctly bulging from the wads of greenbacks,' wrote Smith of their encounter. ' "You might get mugged?" I suggested diffidently. He looked at me as if I was talking about someone stealing candy from a kid, he held up that big fist of his and remarked: "No one is goin' to take the money off old 'Blue' . . . just no one." Patting his concealed pocket, he added: "It stays here . . . until I get home . . . right back inside my own front door!" '

Lewis and Ali got every cent of their purses, and the real brunt of the financial disaster appears to have been borne by the Williams & Glyn Bank. According to unconfirmed reports, the official who vouched for Butty Sugrue's creditworthiness had a stroke soon after the fight and died. Estimates of how much money Sugrue personally lost on the venture vary but the most common figure is somewhere around £20,000. Still, many who worked on the promotion were summoned to his flat in Sean McDermott Street later that week and were paid their wages out of a plastic bag full of cash. This is a side of the story not often told because Sugrue's involvement in Ali–Lewis has been impugned a little by history.

Certainly, the promotion was a financial failure but how much of that was Sugrue's fault? He had brought the single most marketable fighter of the twentieth century to Dublin to take on a credible opponent at a venue where the sightlines from even the cheapest seats were excellent. Despite a relentless publicity campaign encompassing every medium available, and a balmy summer's evening, the public just didn't turn up. Maybe the old story about Dublin not being a city that supports professional boxing rang true. Perhaps the good weather kept a few thousand who might have made the trip otherwise engaged. Who knows? The only thing we can say for definite is that Sugrue did achieve something remarkable by getting Ali to Ireland.

Remember, this was not a fighter way past his sell-by date, picking up money for nothing to feather his retirement nest. This was Ali at thirty years of age. This was Ali before the Rumble in the Jungle, before the Thrilla in Manila. After the summer of 1972, he only grew in stature inside and outside of the ring, and Sugrue's ambition and entrepreneurial spirit ensured Dublin could always boast of hosting one of his fights. It might not have been a bout worthy of being labelled the Collision in Croke Park or anything but it took place principally because one Kerryman dared to dream a little big. For this crime, Sugrue is often ridiculed and lampooned by people who know little of what went into the planning and production of Ali–Lewis.

Four years after that pulsating week in Dublin, Sugrue was lifting a heavy fridge up some stairs at the Wellington when that immense heart, that previously indefatigable organ which withstood so much pressure during all those feats of strength, finally gave out.

Conrad went back to New York claiming he had been left a mere $6,000 out of pocket. His next major promotion was Evel Knievel's abortive attempt to jump Snake River Canyon in Idaho, but it was boxing that continued to consume him. Before Ali's third fight with Ken Norton at Yankee Stadium in 1976, he stayed in Conrad's apartment in the city and when *Dear Muffo* was published in 1982, *Rolling Stone* ran a profile of him under the headline THE HIPPEST GUY IN THE ROOM. Conrad suffered a minor stroke while in Las Vegas for the first Mike Tyson and

Donovan 'Razor' Ruddock bout in 1991, and died shortly after that from a brain tumour.

Like Frazier, Foreman and Liston, Norton is one of those fighters inextricably bound up in the Ali legend. Their names are mentioned in the same breath as his, evoking similar, wonderful memories of a glorious age. But Ali fought sixty-one times between 1960 and 1981. What of the other forty-six men who shared the ring with him? They are among the footnotes of sports history, one-line entries on the most storied CV in all of boxing. For some, their names were read into the record almost as they were led from the stage, and by the time the wrapping had been removed from their hands, obscurity was beckoning with its crooked finger.

Tunney Hunsaker was the first professional boxer to take on the then Cassius Clay. They went six rounds at Louisville's Freedom Hall on 29 October 1960 before a partisan crowd of 6,000, the majority of whom had come to cheer on the home-town kid. Clay won the decision, Hunsaker returned to life as a lawman and served as chief of police in Fayetteville, West Virginia, for more than three decades. At the other end of the life cycle, Trevor Berbick, the Jamaican-born fighter who defeated an ageing Ali in his last fight, did jail time for raping his family's babysitter. Between those two extremes, there are a wealth of other stories reflecting the usual variety of fates that befall retired fighters.

Six years after taking Ali as far as the fifteenth round at Madison Square Garden on 7 December 1970, Oscar Bonavena was shot dead outside the gates of the Mustang Ranch brothel in Las Vegas; the Argentinian had been seeing the wife of the establishment's owner Joe Conforte. In the same city – where far too many fighters seem to wash up – Ron Lyle used the modicum of fame enjoyed by somebody who once lost a 1975 world heavyweight title bout to Ali to spend two decades as a security guard around the casinos. A year after Lyle, Richard Dunn had his shot at the big time. The six-foot-four fair-haired scaffolder from Bradford lasted less than five rounds in Munich's

Olympiahalle. By the mid eighties, Dunn was working on an oil rig in the North Sea when he fell forty feet and broke both his legs.

In the waiting room of Dr Stuart Kirschenbaum's clinic in Detroit, Al 'Blue' Lewis is sitting with his son Alvin. When he stands up to greet you, he is still a huge man, albeit one bulging slightly at the waist. His hair is receding, a salt-and-pepper moustache veers off down each side of his mouth, and behind thick square glasses his right eye is almost shut. We walk to an office at the back of the building to talk. Opening his anorak, he folds his enormous frame into the chair, rubs his hand self-consciously along the top of his head and in a voice so soft and low that it barely registers on the tape recorder, prepares to fill in the blanks about the twenty-nine and a half years since he went toe to toe with Ali.

'You come all the way from Ireland just to see me?'

'No, I live in New York.'

'But you come from Ireland right?'

'Originally, yes.'

'And you like Ireland?'

'Yeah, I like Ireland.'

'Me too, man. I love that place.'

'Really?'

'Oh yeah. As a matter of fact I always wanted to go back and visit. I used to tell my wife that. Used to tell her: "I'm going to take you and show you Ireland." I had one good time over there. Used to tell her: "It's a beautiful, beautiful place." I always told my wife I wanted to bring her there to show her how beautiful it is. I might still bring her on vacation . . . some day.'

His voice trails off slightly with that remark and he bows his head. After nearly thirty years of marriage, Al and Patricia have recently separated and he's taking it badly.

'I appreciate you coming down here to see me.'

'You kiddin' me,' he says, immediately perking up again. 'I wanted to come, man.'

'Yeah?'

'Oh yeah, I love talking about that fight. I loved talking about that week, that was a week when I was somebody.'

'Do you remember much about the fight itself?'

'Shit, yeah, I think about it all the time. It was the biggest day of my life, at least the biggest day before I got married, and as a matter of fact, it prepared me for getting married!'

By way of establishing he has done his homework in advance of our meeting, he assures me that the tape of the fight is still in his son's VCR. His son has accompanied him to the interview and is outside waiting.

'So is that Alvin Junior?'

'No, that's just Alvin, there's another Alvin Junior.'

He chuckles again. For fear of being accused of aping George Foreman's tendency to name all his kids George, he goes on to explain.

'I had this Alvin first but I didn't know I had him. His momma was a woman I knew way back and she gave birth when I came home from the Ali fight. But I didn't know he was my son or my blood for a long time. You know the way it is around here, the mother has the baby, the father's a maybe. But when my wife had twins and one of them was a boy, we named him Alvin Junior. Anyway, Alvin's momma's dead now and since I got separated I'm living with him. He's a good boy.'

The other Alvin, the Junior, is working his way through college and his daughter Erika has already graduated, their progress through the education system a source of immense pride for their father. They were the first Lewis children ever to finish high school and he compared the sight of them walking across the stage at graduation to the excitement he felt fighting Ali. Every time he discusses his current domestic situation, though, his face clouds over a little and his laughter sounds a tad hollow. It's a subject about which he is philosophical.

'I treat folk like I find them, I believe in human beings, I believe in a Supreme Being too, I believe in a God, believe that everything happens for a reason. Any time I've ever had bad luck, I can see where I got it from, why it was happening to me;

sooner or later, everything's meant to be. I'm having a bit of bad luck right now and I can't figure out why, but sooner or later, I will and then I'll ask God for his forgiveness. I go to church regular, used to sing in the choir before I separated from my wife. Ain't been in three or four weeks but I'll go back.'

Arriving home to Detroit that summer of 1972, Al was rich. Not rich like the Ford family who made the town or anything, but he had in his possession $35,000. That was damn rich for a boy who six years earlier thought he wouldn't see the outside world until well into middle-age. He had prospects too. Any fighter who went eleven rounds with the champ was a viable entity in pro boxing. What promoter doesn't want to have somebody on the bill who'd been in with the greatest? It didn't make him box office like Frazier and those guys, just gave him a degree of credibility, something to bargain with when negotiating a fee.

He was full of good intentions too. Inside a prison cell, a man learns a lot about the value of things. Al had waited years for his big pay day and he didn't intend wasting the cash. He'd seen and heard too many stories about people being fools with money. This was the sort of capital he could do something with. So he did. Figuring he owed his momma something for the pain and anguish he'd caused her all those years earlier, he plunked down a portion of money on a house for his parents. The first house ever owned by a member of Lewis family. Under the circumstances, what more could a man possibly do? Now that you ask.

'Verner was my mother. She never owned a home before until I came back from fighting Ali and bought her that one. It was a few blocks down the street from here. On Lensdale Street, that was where the house was. It was a funny thing though. I bought her the house, bought her all new furniture for the house. Then one time I came in and she was talking to her best friend on the phone, and I was listening and thought she was bragging on me. But no, turns out she was bragging on my older brother who was a dope fiend. He'd bought her a pair of gloves or something.

Couldn't believe it. That kind of hurt my feelings. She was talking about that dope fiend, she was so proud of him for those gloves.'

If that's the sort of thing which makes a body wonder why he bothers, Al had plenty of reasons to remain cheerful. There was Patricia for starters. He met her when they sang together in the choir at St James' Baptist Church over on the east side. Between, and sometimes even during hymns, they used to check each other out, an unlikely pair drawn together in God's house. The boxing ex-con and the smart teacher who would eventually become head of the foreign-language department in the city's public schools system.

'We hit it off, we just hit it off some way. I remember looking back to see if she was looking back and she was looking to see if I was looking. You know how it is.'

A month after Al came back from Dublin, they were married. He had some money behind him and the chance to earn some more before he finished in the ring. There'd hardly be many five-figure purses like the one he'd just had but, approaching thirty, he was confident he could bring home a couple of decent-sized cheques without risking injury. That plan ran aground pretty quick, however. After the pomp and ceremony of a week sharing the limelight with Ali in a far-off land, it was difficult to get motivated for good old club fights. He didn't get back in the ring until 22 January 1973, winning the decision after ten rounds against Charlie Reno. It was the kind of fight he'd have finished early a couple of years before. The warning signs were already there.

Six weeks later, Jack O'Halloran took full advantage of his complacency. It went the distance and Al couldn't complain when the judges chose against him. Matter of fact, their decision almost convinced him to quit altogether. He'd figured he'd give it one more real shot before hanging them up for good. On 19 July, a year to the day since his encounter with Ali, he travelled to Halifax, Nova Scotia, and dropped Claude McBride in the third. Jimmy Cross was dispatched in similar fashion in

Oklahoma City on 4 September and when J.D. McAuley lasted only as far as the second in Dayton on 14 November, it appeared there might just be something left in the tank yet. None of his opponents were exactly world-beaters but wins were wins. Maybe he was on the way back.

A few weeks later, on one of those unforgiving Detroit mornings when the cold seeps right into your bones, Al came upon a Catholic priest shivering outside the Brewster gym, complaining he couldn't get his car to start. He stopped to help because that was the kind of thing he liked to do. The former teenage terror was always anxious to be a stand-up guy. Al had his head in the engine of the car when the battery blew up in his face. His right eye took the brunt of it. The retina was detached and eventually the eye would almost close. No sight. No boxing. No more pay days. With the stoicism forged inside the walls of Jackson State, he came to terms with it more easily than most.

'That was it for me and boxing but, you know, I needed to retire anyway. That was for the best, I always said I'd retire after the Ali fight but once you get offered money to fight you always want to come back.'

Anyway, the fact that a man couldn't box didn't mean he was lost to boxing. Not in Detroit, one of the most fecund breeding grounds of all for the sport. Al found a job in the laundry of Huntzel Hospital and headed back to Brewster to work on the other side of the ropes in his spare time. Best of all, he embraced the new role with a heartfelt belief he could do more than teach the fundamentals of ring craft. He wanted to make a difference in people's lives, figuring that the opportunity to train properly might prevent a few kids from going astray. Who better to teach them than a reformed ex-con?

'First, I've got to get all their minds,' said Lewis in a 1997 interview with the *Detroit Free Press* where he outlined his philosophy. 'You've got to be equipped to be a good fighter, a champion boxer. If you don't have the mind for it, you'll be down in the ring. So first of all, I get into their schooling. They have to be able to think so they can be able to use their brain. A lot of them try to come in and fight like I did. I didn't want to learn nothing at first. They come here and they just want to beat up some kids. I have to teach them there's more to it than that.

'Kids don't want to learn. They've got too many things like drugs, like cigarettes, like robbing; they have babies and are on welfare. They have bad things calling out to them all the time. You've got these kids crying out for help but you've got to reach out to get them. They're crying out for help all the time. A lot of times they ain't got no choice. Some can't go to school. They're doing the same things that I was doing when I was a kid and it's going to happen to their great-great-grandkids, and their great-great-great-grandkids if they don't want to live another life.

'When they explain their situation to me, I tell them my story. You know they all come from big families too, they ain't bad kids, they just come from bad situations. I tell them my story about fighting Ali, tell them: "I came up just like you kids, poor, black, hungry and dirty and I didn't realise my mistakes until I was in prison." I tell them they can realise earlier than I did that they should stay in school, I was in prison before I realised that. I warn them: "Boxing isn't for everybody, not everybody can box." It's tough, man, but that's been my programme ever since I came home from prison.'

The only times Lewis ever went back to Jackson State Prison were in his capacity as boxing trainer. Fulfilling a promise he'd made to people in the jail, he brought some of his charges up to fight. When he was inside, he remembered how much it meant to have a few hours of distraction like a boxing tournament against outsiders. Anything to help pass the livelong day. If the prison visits made him feel good about how far he'd come, seeing the place frightened the pants off his fighters. Well, some more than others.

In 1979, when Lewis had been training youngsters for nearly six years, Corey Johnson crossed his path for the first time. A brazen, cheeky seven-year-old, already too well acquainted with trouble, he immediately recognised much of his younger self in this street urchin with attitude. Saving this boy from himself became a personal mission and oh, it wasn't easy. Johnson wasn't one of those impressionable kids who frighten quick. It took some serious work, and a lot of time and patience to convince him that he could use his energy in a more positive fashion. It wasn't until Corey turned twelve that Lewis knew for sure the child had seen the error of his ways and preferred boxing to street-fighting. By then he'd invested five years in his redemption.

Johnson cut a swathe through amateur boxing, winning Junior Golden Gloves, Junior Olympics and Diamond Gloves. Then he turned pro, and eschewing the opportunity to move across town to the international boxing landmark, the Kronk Gym, he stayed with the man who turned him on to the sport and changed his life. Through twenty victories in his first twenty-one fights, Johnson earned the nickname 'Prime Time', and in March 1996, the southpaw welterweight's twenty-second professional bout was on the undercard of Wayne McCullough–Jose Luis Bueno at the Point Depot in Dublin. Nearly quarter of a century after fighting Ali, Al 'Blue' Lewis returned to Ireland as a trainer.

'It was different going back as a trainer. When I went there as a boxer, I had everything given to me, I was real important, man. I was treated very well all the way up to when I left. I didn't know much about Ireland. In fact, I knew nothing about Ireland really, I had heard it was a nice place but I had no idea I'd be treated as well as I was. It was different when I went with Johnson, I was just there.'

For somebody just there, he made his presence felt. During Johnson's ten-round draw with Australian Shannon Taylor, Lewis was reprimanded by the referee Fred Tiedt for shouting and coaching excessively from the corner.

'Al is great as a trainer, a beautiful person, smart, knows the fundamentals of the game,' said Corey Johnson that week in Dublin. 'People don't give him that much credit but I've been with him for seventeen years, it's going on eighteen years, and I know Al better than anyone and he's smart fighter, a smart teacher. The way he trains is incredible. He keeps the meanness in you, the dog in you. You know what I'm saying? I promise you I will be world champion. I will be Al's living dream, world champion, something he didn't do.'

Two months later, Johnson was knocked out in the fourth round of his attempt to win the IBF junior welterweight title off Kostya Tszyu, and the relationship between fighter and trainer began to unravel. No longer involved in training fighters, Ali is still hurt by that break-up, offering only this when questioned about what happened between them.

'I started him off in boxing but he got too bigshot for me. I'm retired from all that now.'

One wall of Dr Kirschenbaum's office is hung with signed limited-edition portraits of Ali by Andy Warhol. They are huge and striking, and valuable too. Everywhere, there is the paraphernalia of a life immersed in the sport. A friend as much as a physician to Lewis, from his own days boxing light-heavy in the New York Golden Gloves to his time as a judge for the World Boxing Council and his eleven-year term as Michigan State Boxing Commissioner, Kirschenbaum has always seen both sides of the fight game. At various junctures in the conversation, an item of the doctor's memorabilia catches Lewis's eye, and sparks a thought.

'I see Muhammad every few years at boxing matches, you know,' he says, running his fingers along a framed photo of his adversary from all those years ago. 'He came here to see his daughter Laila box at Cobo Hall a couple of years ago. That was the last time I saw him. We didn't really have a chance to talk. I spoke to him for a few minutes before her fight and he put his arms out for a big hug. I see him every few years, we always hug.'

Men who have met inside the ropes enjoy a unique camaraderie. Sometimes, most often in the event of lingering feuds, it goes unspoken but it is always there. When Lewis talks of Ali though, there is so much explicit affection in his voice. Before they fought, he felt thankful towards Ali for giving him the opportunity to participate in a fight that would yield him the biggest wage of his life. These times, he feels equally grateful for the memory.

'I watched the fight the other day and I can appreciate it more now. For a long time, I was ashamed of that fight. People would say: "You did well 'Blue'," but to me I didn't. Now I look at it and I can relate to it better. I can understand where I came from and how I got to be in the ring with Ali. I appreciate that journey now. I suppose because I'm nearly sixty years old I can appreciate it all a bit better, I mean, Ali was the best amateur, the best professional and heavyweight champ so many times over.

'If I had started out earlier, I would have been a lot better. I would have had the experience that people like Ali did. I never fought as a kid, never fought amateur like I should have. If I'd have fought more from an early age, I would have been able to defend myself better. It fascinates me now that I think I did OK when for so long I was ashamed of how I fought that night. I felt that I fought a coward's fight. Now I look at it and compare it with other guys who fought him and I think I did excellent. I lost but I didn't look like no punk in losing.

'Now I think more that I was the Mayor of Detroit and that's good but Ali was like the President of the United States of America and that's better. He was the champ and I figured it was my chance of getting to be champ, but it wasn't. Ali don't hit that hard but he hit me so many times. He doesn't miss much. He's not like a George Foreman-type puncher but he's so scientific about it and then he doesn't get hit himself. I was used to boxing regular boxers, you hit them and they hit you, with Ali, he hits you but then you can't hit him, he just don't get hit. I was trying to take his crown but he just don't get hit.

'I thought I had a chance. I'm a dog and I figured it was my turn. I went there to win. I wanted to beat Ali bad. Ali was the best in the world, and me, I wanted to be the best in the world too, I wanted to be on top. I tried hard but I wasn't good enough, every time I gotta chance, I tried, I tried everything I had. I wanted bad to become the one the crowd comes to see instead of coming to see him. Whenever I fought here in Detroit, people came just to see me – they didn't come to see my opponent, it was all me. I wanted to be like Ali, wanted people to come to see me fight wherever I went.'

Apart from when discussing his marital problems, there is no great longing in his voice when he speaks. No sense that he thinks he could have done more in that fight in particular or in life in general. He doesn't moan about the hand life dealt him, in fact, he regards everything that happened to him after leaving prison on 7 January 1966 as a massive bonus. There were twelve Lewis brothers. Al is the only one of them still alive and none of the others lived to see the ripe old age of fifty-nine, the birthday he celebrated the week after we met.

'I ain't got no regrets. You got to remember I came through the back door. I'd read about Sonny Liston and what he did when I was in prison. So I figured I might be able to do what he did and I had a chance to taste it. I came from nowhere. I ain't got a high school diploma or nothing but I had a chance to taste it. I need a job right now but my son is looking after me OK and I'm feeling pretty good. I got my memories too . . . and God will bless me with more yet.'

He smacks his right fist off his left hand for emphasis, pauses for a moment and then returns to a familiar theme.

'I do love Ireland though, they treated me like I was somebody over there. Like I was somebody.'

He repeats that same mantra again and again, the memory of his week in the sun warming him still.

Bibliography

Ali, Muhammad and Durham, Richard: *The Greatest*, Random House, New York, 1975

Brynner, Rock: *Yul: The Man Who Would Be King*, Simon and Schuster, 1989

Conrad, Harold: *Dear Muffo*, Stein and Day, New York, 1982

Conteh, John: *I Conteh*, Harrap, London, 1982

Deford, Frank: *The World's Tallest Midget*, Little, Brown, Boston, 1987

Dundee, Angelo: *I Only Talk Winning*, Contemporary Books, Chicago, 1985

Early, Gerald: *I'm a Little Bit Special*, Yellow Jersey Press, London, 1999

Early, Gerald: *The Culture of Bruising*, Ecco Press, New Jersey, 1994

Gorn, Elliott J: *Ali: The People's Champ*, University of Illinois Press, Chicago, 1995

Gorn, Elliot J: *The Manly Art*, Cornell University Press, New York, 1994

Gleeson, John: *Fyffes' Dictionary of Irish Sporting Greats*, Etta Place, Dublin, 1993

Grobel, Lawrence: *The Hustons*, Cooper Square Press, New York, 2000

Hauser, Thomas: *Muhammad Ali – His Life and Times*, Pan Books, London, 1992

Miller, Kerby: *Emigrants and Exiles*, Oxford University Press, New York, 1985

Monaghan, Paddy: *The Sunshine in my Life*, Tony Williams Publications, Taunton, 1993

Pacheco, Ferdie: *The Fight Doctor*, Birch Lane Press, New York, 1992

Schulberg, Budd: *Loser and Still Champion*, Doubleday, New York, 1972

Shecter, Leonard: *The Jocks*, Paperback Library, New York, 1971

Smith, Raymond: *Urbi et Orbi and All That*, Mount Cross, Dublin, 1995

Strathmore, William: *Muhammad Ali – The Unseen Archives*, Paragon, Bath, 2001

Stravinsky, John: *Muhammad Ali*, Park Lane Press, New York, 1997

Taub, Michael: *Jack Doyle: Fighting for Love*, Stanley Paul, London, 1990

Tobin, Fergal: *The Best of Decades, Ireland in the 1960s*, Gill and Macmillan, Dublin, 1996

Newspapers and Periodicals
The Irish Independent, Sunday Independent, Irish Press, Cork Examiner, Irish Times, The Sunday Tribune, The Sun, Daily Mail, The New York Times, New York Daily News, The Times, The Ring, Detroit Free Press, Detroit News, Playboy

Television Programmes
Muhammad Ali versus Cathal O'Shannon – John Condon, producer, RTE, 1972

Mono: Programme 7 – Colm O'Callaghan, producer, RTE 2001